Bradford Railways in Colour
Volume 3: The L&YR and GNR Lines After Steam

Willowherb Publishing

First published 2021

Willowherb Publishing
www.willowherbpublishing.co.uk

© Alan Whitaker and Jan Rapacz 2021

The right of Alan Whitaker and Jan Rapacz to be identified as the authors of this work has been asserted by them in accordance with the Copyright, Design and Patents Act 1988.

All rights reserved. No part of this book may be reproduced, or utilised in any form, stored or introduced into a retrieval system, or transmitted in any form or by any means (electronic, mechanical, photocopying, recording or otherwise) without prior permission from the Publishers.

Printed in the UK by:
The Amadeus Press
Cleckheaton
BD19 4TQ
ISBN: 978-0-9935678-7-2

Front Cover
A regular visitor to Bradford in the 1960s and 70s was Deltic No. 55020 *Nimbus* (originally numbered D9020) seen here climbing towards Laisterdyke with nine coaches in tow on the 1155 Bradford Exchange to London King's Cross on 18 May 1977. The industrial landscape of this part of the city is well illustrated with a demolition clearance site on one side of the railway and a scrap yard on the other. *(John S. Whiteley)*

Frontispiece
A quiet interlude at Bradford Exchange station in the summer of 1972 finds 'Peak' Class 45 diesel No. 16 taking a rest before its next duty. With only six months left before closure, the once elegant Victorian station presents a sorry sight. The sleepers piled up on the right had just been removed from one of the five former Lancashire & Yorkshire Railway platforms which had been abandoned, with all remaining services concentrated on the ex-Great Northern side of the station. *(David Christie)*

Rear Cover
Class 47 No. 47288 carefully eases out of Springmill Street goods yard with the previous day's scrap train from McIntyre's at Laisterdyke which it would work to Healey Mills, near Wakefield, pending onward transit of the load to South Yorkshire. *(Andrew Rapacz)*

Introduction

The decimation of railway services in the Bradford area in the 1950s and 1960s was ruthless and often ill-considered. By the time British Rail withdrew its last steam locomotives in August 1968, there wasn't a great deal left to close but BR was still under Government pressure to cut costs so the hatchet men returned to tidy up the loose ends.

By the mid-1980s, Bradford had lost all but its passenger lines from Interchange and Forster Square stations and two private freight sidings serving scrap metal recycling firms at Laisterdyke and Shipley.

This book is the third in the *Bradford Railways in Colour* series of albums from Willowherb Publishing and focuses on what has happened on the city's former Lancashire & Yorkshire and Great Northern lines in the half century since the demise of steam.

In 1968, these lines started out from the magnificent Victorian citadel that was Bradford Exchange station. It was replaced by a much smaller facility in 1973 and belatedly renamed Bradford Interchange ten years later. The old station was swept away, along with the buildings and warehouses of the neighbouring Bridge Street Goods Depot which provided the site for the Bradford Interchange bus station and underground garage.

The city's status as a major railway centre was already in decline by 1968 and BR's decision to replace the original 10-platform grand terminal with a four-platform configuration tells its own story. On the other side of the city centre, Forster Square station has also been replaced by a more modest facility but that has seen a renaissance thanks to investment in electrification in the 1990s. The changes on the former Midland Railway line out of Bradford Forster Square since 1968 will be highlighted in *Bradford Railways in Colour Volume 4*, which is in preparation.

In the period covered by this book, Bradford lost its last locomotive depot, its last goods yards, the last remnants of its branch lines, its last carriage sidings and many of its direct its long distance services. However, it did get two new central termini – albeit smaller than their predecessors – and several new suburban stations, including Low Moor which opened in 2017 and is, so far, the only one on the south side of the city to have been restored to the network. Most of the new stations were expensive replacements for short-sighted closures in the 1960s when BR found cost-cutting easier than developing its existing local business.

The former L&YR and GNR lines out of Bradford are now perceived as the poor relations of the city's much-changed railway landscape but things have stabilised over the last 30 years which is a welcome relief after the upheavals of the previous decades.

Although this book concentrates on events after the end of steam on the national network in August 1968, it should be noted that Bradford had lost its last steam locomotive depot a year earlier with the closure of the former L&YR Low Moor shed in 1967. The other steam depot on the south side of the city was the former Great Northern shed at Bowling which made national headlines when it became one of the earliest pioneers of dieselisation on British Railways.

Bowling received its first allocation of brand new diesel rail cars in 1954, a year before BR published its 'Modernisation Plan' which set out its blueprint for the future of the industry. The main objective was to replace steam with diesel and electric traction as quickly as possible and to close unprofitable lines and services. The aim 'to make the railways pay' was a slogan dreamed up by the hierarchy to satisfy the Treasury and it was doomed from the start.

The proposed timescales were wildly unrealistic and BR continued to lose money, partly due to its heavy investment in a myriad of hastily-ordered and untested diesel locomotive types, some of which were so unreliable that they barely out lasted the steam locomotives they were built to replace. But there were success stories too and some first generation diesel locomotives and railcars went on to have long careers, once BR engineers had managed to get a grip with their initial teething troubles. Some of those early types, which gave years of excellent service before being gradually replaced by more modern traction, are featured in this book.

As one of the country's first diesel maintenance depots, the old Bowling shed was modernised and renamed Hammerton Street. It was one of the jewels in BR's crown in the 1950s as the successful development of diesel passenger trains progressed. The depot continued in service until 1984 when its operations were transferred to Leeds.

The former Great Northern lines and stations in the Bradford area took a hammering between nationalisation of Britain's railways in 1948 and the end of steam 20 years later. The first major closure came in 1955 when the lines from Bradford to Halifax and Keighley via Queensbury closed to passengers. Although initially retained for freight, both lines were severed as through routes a year later, leaving the remaining goods depots on a hiding to nothing. At the Bradford end of the Queensbury lines, a short stub to Horton Park and City Road made it into the 1970s and these locations are featured in their last weeks of operation in 1972. The main line to Wakefield via Dudley Hill, and the branch from Tyersal Junction to Pudsey Greenside, also succumbed before the end of steam but goods to Dudley Hill survived until 1981.

The last remaining part of the former Great Northern line between Laisterdyke and Shipley (Windhill) has managed to scrape into this book as it outlived the steam age by two months. Although the through line closed in 1964, the section between Shipley and Idle was still open for goods until October 1968. Another long lost ex-GN line in the Bradford area to survive the end of steam was the Laisterdyke to Bowling Junction avoiding line used by trains between Leeds and Halifax which did not need to call at Exchange station. It was closed to passengers in 1969 - and as a through route a year later - but hung on for freight to Laisterdyke until 1985.

Stations and goods depots on the former L&YR main line also fell by the wayside in the 1950s and 60s, with Bowling Junction and Wyke & Norwood Green stations the first to go. By 1968, there were no intermediate stations between Bradford and Halifax but the former L&Y goods depot at Springmill Street survived until 1984.

With 112 pages available, this book can only provide a glimpse into what has happened on Bradford's former L&Y and GNR lines in the last 53 years but all the principal changes have been covered. Although we have brought the story up to date, we have concentrated mainly on scenes and locations which can no longer be witnessed.

Once again, we are indebted to all the photographers who have willingly and generously allowed us to reproduce their work and also to the contributors who provided additional information to enhance the narrative.

Alan Whitaker

September 2021

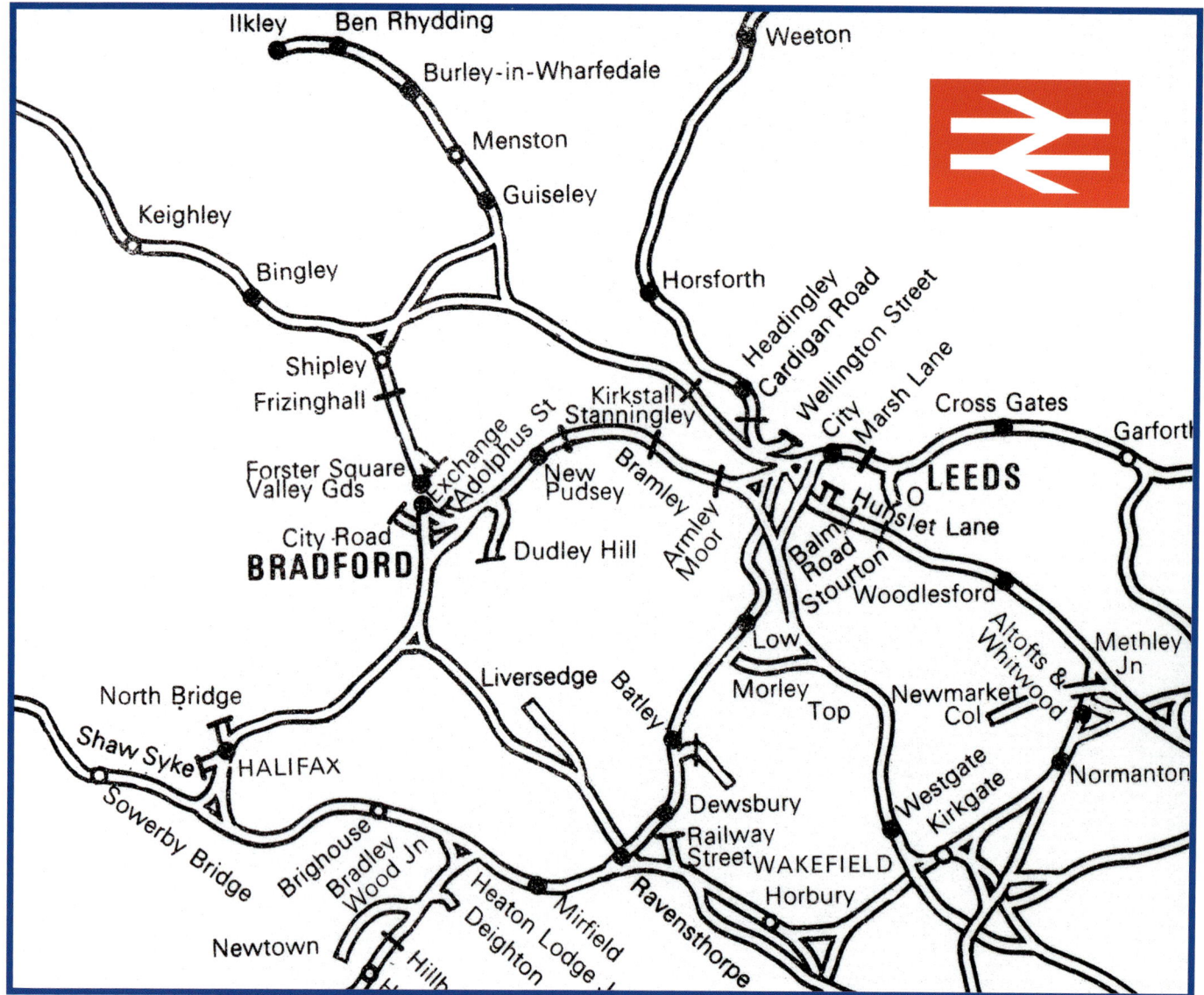

Extract from an updated British Rail System Map dated 5 May 1969 and showing the lines still in use for passenger and freight traffic at the time. Rail freight in the Bradford area had been much diminished by closures in the 1950s and 60s but the goods depots at Adolphus Street, Dudley Hill, City Road and Valley Road were still operating. Also still open in 1969 were Laisterdyke (East) and Springmill Street yards but these seem to have been omitted from the diagram due to lack of space. *(British Rail)*

The view from the concourse at Bradford Exchange on 24 June 1972 as a Class 110 Birmingham Railway Carriage & Wagon 'Calder Valley' diesel multiple unit set powers up in Platform 7 at the start of its journey to Blackpool. The usual three-car formation has been supplemented with the addition of a Metropolitan Cammell trailer car, conspicuous by its shallower windows. The first Class 110 units were delivered to Bradford Hammerton Street diesel depot in 1961 and spearheaded a new era of improved Trans-Pennine services linking major population centres such as York, Harrogate, Wakefield, Leeds, Bradford, Manchester and Liverpool. All 30 sets in the fleet were subsequently based at Hammerton Street where they remained until its closure in 1984. By the time of this view, passengers had become accustomed to the station platforms being much lighter, following the removal of a large number of glass roof panels as a safety precaution. The work began in November 1968 and took about 10 weeks to complete. Although this gave the station an air of semi-dereliction, the magnificence of the wrought ironwork which formed the twin arches of the roof could still be appreciated. *(David Christie)*

Bradford had a long history of direct passenger services to the West Country with famous trains such as *The Cornishman* to Penzance and *The Devonian* to Paignton featuring in the timetable for decades. Until May 1967, these ran from Forster Square station but were then transferred to start at Exchange. Bathed by late afternoon sun, Leeds Holbeck's Class 46 No. 186 waits at Platform 6 with the 1705 Saturdays only train to Bristol Temple Meads on 18 September 1971. This service started from Leeds on weekdays. The locomotive was transferred to Bristol not long after this photo was taken and stayed on the Western Region for 11 years before returning to the Eastern Region for its final year in service. It was withdrawn in December 1982 after a service life of just over 20 years. Vestiges of the steam age still proliferate across the station, as highlighted by the elderly Lancashire & Yorkshire Railway 'parachute' water tank and various early 1950s British Railways enamel signage. *(D J Mitchell)*

BR Class 03 No. 2371 stands alongside Bradford Exchange station at the top end of the Vicar Lane carriage sidings while on pilot duties in 1969. The short wheelbase of these small 0-6-0 diesel shunters meant that they were frequently coupled to a 4-wheel match wagon, as seen here, to ensure that track circuits would be activated. This particular locomotive, which was destined to become a local 'celebrity' later in its career, was transferred to Bradford Hammerton Street shed in September 1968 and stayed until March 1973 when it was reallocated to Healey Mills. After a few months there, it went to York then returned to Hammerton Street in 1976 where it remained until transfer back to York, and subsequently Gateshead, in 1983. Built at Swindon in 1958, 2371 had started life in BR's Departmental pool as Dep. 92 and was based at Chesterton Junction, Cambridge, for nine years. It was taken into the main BR fleet in 1967 and fitted with dual brakes.
(Willowherb Publishing Collection)

This view of Bradford Exchange, taken from Bridge Street on 10 April 1971, shows Leeds Holbeck's BR Sulzer Type 2 (Class 24) No. 5147 which has propelled empty coaches into Platform 8. These would form *The Devonian* express to Paignton, which the Class 24 would work as far as Leeds where it would be replaced by a 'Peak' Type 4. A month later, this formerly prestigious train was rescheduled to start and terminate at Leeds, thereby further diminishing Bradford's importance on the national network. Things would get much worse in the years to come. On the far left, a rake of Pullman stock occupies Platform 1 while Platform 10 on the opposite side of the station hosts another BR Sulzer Type 2 on the Bradford portion of a London King's Cross service. More coaching stock can be seen in the Vicar Lane carriage sidings on the far right of the photograph. These sidings occupied the site of the Lancashire & Yorkshire Railway Company's original goods depot in central Bradford. However, it was far too small to cope with a huge increase in traffic in the 1870s and a new, much larger depot was built at nearby Bridge Street, opening in stages between 1880 and the mid-1890s. *(Peter Fitton)*

The skeletal framework of the Bradford Exchange station train shed roof over Platforms 1 to 5 is well illustrated in this view taken from the far end of Platform 5 on 7 September 1971. This had been the Lancashire & Yorkshire Railway's side of the station after it was enlarged to facilitate the Great Northern Railway Company's trains from 1886. Each company had five platforms, with the GNR operating out of Platforms 6 to 10. All five platforms in this view were taken out of use on 21 February 1972. This enabled track and associated signalling to be removed so construction of the first part of the new Bradford Exchange station on the other side of Bridge Street could begin. Having been allowed to deteriorate by British Railways during the 1950s and 60s, the station building was in urgent need of an expensive facelift which never came. Instead, BR concentrated its efforts on Leeds and Bradford's place on the national network became terminally weakened as more and more services were taken away. *(Stuart Baker)*

The Lancashire & Yorkshire Railway's Bridge Street Goods Depot occupied a prime city centre site and was one of Bradford's busiest rail yards for more than 70 years. However, it fell victim to 'rationalisation' of goods facilities in the area and closed in 1962, with its traffic being transferred to other local depots. Although all the sidings had been lifted, the main warehouses and offices stood empty for years until the site was identified for redevelopment as a new rail and bus Transport Interchange, about which more later. This is the scene at Bridge Street not long before demolition began in 1968. The outlines of some of the sidings can still be discerned years after the rails were lifted. *(John Holroyd)*

On 8 February 1972, a Leeds-bound Metropolitan Cammell DMU starts the climb out of Bradford Exchange past the mechanical signalbox which controlled train movements into and out of the station, as well as the adjoining Vicar Lane carriage sidings. A legacy of the time when L&YR and GNR trains had their own platforms meant that the station was still controlled by separate lever frames, with trains only able to cross over at Mill Lane further up the line. The lattice girder bridge carrying Bridge Street over the railway was deemed life expired and would soon be removed and replaced by an embankment when the old Exchange station was superseded by a new smaller station in 1973. Note the platform number indicators showing an impending arrival at Platform 5 on the approach line to the left of the signalbox. *(John Holroyd)*

The Saturday service from Weymouth to Bradford nears the end of its long journey from the Dorset Coast with English Electric Type 4 (Class 40) No. D348 in charge on 1 July 1972. The train is passing the crossovers between the former L&YR and GNR routes at Mill Lane Junction but the rusty rails in the foreground indicate that part of the network of lines into Exchange station were already out of use. The line to the right is a long 'through' siding which had run from Bowling Junction to the Bridge Street goods depot but, by this time, was only used to facilitate entry into the former L&YR yards at Springmill Street (off Manchester Road) and the Broomfield Coal Sidings. The late 1960s and early 1970s was an era of transition for locomotive and coaching stock liveries as corporate blue and grey took over. The Class 40 seen here is clinging on to its original green livery but with the addition of a full yellow front-end warning panel. This adornment, which started to appear towards the end of 1966, did not suit some classes but safety for railway staff, such as trackside workers, was more important than aesthetics. Locos with full yellow ends could be seen approaching from greater distances, thereby potentially saving lives. *(Peter Fitton)*

Following removal of the lines on the L&YR side of Exchange station, preparatory work for the demolition of the Bridge Street bridge was quickly implemented. All services in and out of the old station were switched over to the former GNR side from 21 February 1972 so ground works for the first half of the replacement station could begin. This required 18,000 cubic yards of tipped material to raise the platform levels 12 feet higher than the lowest point of the former Bridge Street goods depot site. Here, Brush Type 4 (Class 47) No. 1517 gets into its stride at the start of the climb from Bradford Exchange on a London train on wet day in the late Spring of 1972. *(Jan Rapacz Collection)*

Work on the first part of the replacement station is well underway in this August 1972 view which shows how the new Platforms 1 & 2 were constructed from prefabricated concrete components. A combined 6-car DMU set, comprising both Class 110 BRCW and Class 101 Metropolitan Cammell units, drifts downgrade towards the old station and is about to pass beneath an impressive signal gantry which was swept away after completion of the new station. The massive retaining wall was typical of the often extensive and heavy civil engineering works that were necessary to facilitate the growth of the railway network across the West Riding in the second half of the 19th century and it is still an instantly recognisable feature on the approach into what is now known as Bradford Interchange station. *(Robert Anderson)*

An unidentified BR Class 03 diesel shunter, coupled to a wooden planked open match wagon, shunts coaching stock into Platform 10 at the old Exchange station while work progresses on construction of the awning for Platforms 1 and 2 of the new station on 12 August 1972. Just beyond, part of the Bridge Street bridge has been removed to facilitate construction of the station's booking hall. On the left, preparatory works for the Transport Interchange are underway. A hoarding on the right is advertising trips to the Belle Vue Zoological Gardens in Manchester, which was a popular destination for visitors from around region for many years until it finally closed its doors in September 1977. *(Stuart Baker)*

With only nine minutes to go before the midnight closure deadline, this is the scene at the old Bradford Exchange station on Saturday, 13 January 1973. It is, perhaps, fitting that the photographers who turned up to record the occasion were presented with the familiar faces of two local Class 110 DMU sets sitting side by side at the stops on Platforms 8 and 9 for the last time. A third Class 110 was to arrive on a late-running service from Manchester just after midnight to bring down the curtain on this iconic 19th century railway terminus. The lines into the station were then quickly severed and trains started using two platforms at the incomplete new 'station' which looked like a building site and was massively off-putting for intending passengers for many weeks to come. *(Stuart Baker)*

The new Exchange station – or, more precisely, what there was of it – opened for business on Sunday 14 January 1973. The following day finds a Class 110 unit occupying one of the two new platforms which had been squeezed in on the north side of the redundant former L&YR signalbox. This dated from 1886 and had closed the previous day. It would soon be demolished to make way for two more platforms. The fact that only four platforms were deemed necessary shows how far Bradford's rail services had declined since the 1950s when 10 platforms were barely enough to accommodate all the trains arriving and departing from the former terminus. Closure of the old station seemed premature, to say the least, as the concourse and some of the offices there had to remain in use for parcels business for about five weeks until the new facility was ready to accommodate it. *(Jan Rapacz Collection)*

This is what happens when local Council 'leaders' with no imagination or foresight sit back and do nothing to try to preserve the heritage of the community they are supposed to represent. The old Bradford Exchange station was a Victorian masterpiece of design and a triumph of execution but it was disgracefully ignored and a golden opportunity to find a new use for it was lost. The G-Mex Centre in Manchester is housed in what was the city's Central station, which closed in 1969. But instead of allowing it to be demolished with indecent haste, local politicians bided their time, secured the required investment and it was re-purposed to become the valuable asset it is today. What Bradford got was an uneven car park made up of crushed rubble and large potholes that were frequently flooded. The eyesore site was eventually redeveloped for the Bradford Crown Court building. This view was captured on Saturday, 14 April 1973 as destruction of the old station was well underway. The much-admired Corinthian-style roof support columns down the centre of the station had been cast at the foundry of local firm Thornton & Crebbin, of Hammerton Street, in 1885. *(Clive Weston)*

Still dwarfed by the towering remnants of the old Bradford Exchange roof arches in the distance, the new station is seen here fully operational in November 1974. The photograph was taken from the Caledonia Street bridge and clearly highlights the simplified track arrangements. The station included an engine release line from Platform 1 which was operated at the terminal end by a 2-lever ground frame known as Bradford 'A.' This was activated from Mill Lane signalbox. A locomotive release crossover was also provided from Platform 2 as part of the final completion works for the station. In this view, a Brush Type 2 (Class 31) No. 31410 is seen waiting to depart on the noon service to London King's Cross. Croft Street bridge, which was removed and replaced as part of the Bradford Ring Road widening scheme in the early 1990s, can be seen crossing the station platforms in the middle distance while, beyond, the familiar backdrop of 1970s Bradford includes the Victoria Hotel, the Valley Road Power Station chimney and other 'modern' buildings in the city centre, some of which have since disappeared from the landscape after a very short history. *(John S. Whiteley)*

From the vantage point of Croft Street bridge, another of the familiar Class 110 DMUs is seen leaving the new Bradford Exchange station on a Manchester Victoria to Leeds service on 18 July 1975. Tucked in the stabling siding alongside the high retaining wall is one of Hammerton Street's 204 horsepower Class 03 diesel shunters with a short rake of parcels vans. The elevated Broomfield coal depot yard, off Britannia Street, with its array of hoppers and other coal handling equipment, can be seen to good effect in this view. Several mineral wagons are also visible in the sidings which closed in September 1976. *(D. J. Mitchell)*

Having been detached from its train, Class 47 No. 47411 prepares to use the crossover between Platforms 2 and 3 to run round on 24 January 1976. It would then work the midday train to London King's Cross. The locomotive, originally numbered D1510, entered service in February 1963 at Finsbury Park depot in North London. Its final allocation was to Immingham from where it was withdrawn in June 1989. After a period in store, it was scrapped in 1994. Some of the hydraulic buffers from the old Exchange station were reused in the new facility. These have since been superseded by more modern friction rail-mounted 'train arresting' buffer stops but the old hydraulic buffers have been retained just behind them. They are set in a permanently compressed position and are a poignant link with the original 10-platform grand terminus. *(Steve Hall)*

On the same day as the view on the previous page, Leeds Holbeck's Class 45 'Peak' No. 45035 had a day out on special duties. It is seen here at the new Bradford Exchange having taken over from a pair of Class 25s for the middle leg of the Locomotive Club of Great Britain's *Pennine Venturer* Rail Tour. The train had set out from Liverpool Lime Street and, after visiting Liverpool Exchange, had travelled via Wigan, Manchester Victoria and Huddersfield to Bradford. After leaving Bradford, the train went to Wakefield, then Harrogate, York, Hebden Bridge, Blackburn and Bolton before finally arriving back in Lime Street via Manchester at 6.46 that evening - only one minute later than the booked time. Derby-built 45035 was new in September 1961 as D44 and was renumbered for BR's computerised Total Operations Processing System (TOPS) in February 1975. It was withdrawn from service in May 1981 and scrapped six months later after a service life of just under 20 years. *(Steve Hall)*

The high 19th century retaining wall which marked the descent into the old Bradford Exchange station for more than a century towers over the toy-like platforms of its modern replacement facility on a wet - and evidently quiet - 14 March 1977. Platform 4 hosts a BRCW Class 110 (bottom left) in front of a Derby-built BR Class 108 two-car set, recently refurbished and repainted from all-over blue into BR's new off-white and blue stripe corporate livery. The unit is standing alongside Class 03 shunter, No. 03089, which is waiting for work on the stabling siding. This siding, which could hold a maximum of nine coaches, was commissioned, along with Platforms 3 and 4, on Sunday, 3 June 1973 – almost five months after the station's official opening. The locomotive entered service at Hammerton Street as D2089 in May 1960 and remained part of the depot's allocation until 1979 when it was transferred to York. It received its TOPS identity in February 1974, becoming 03089. After withdrawal from service in 1987, it was bought for preservation and is now based at the Mangapps Railway Museum in Essex. *(Steve Hall)*

A busier scene at Bradford Exchange as Deltic No. 55007 *Pinza* erupts into action at the head of the 1740 service to London King's Cross on 4 August 1977. Like its namesake - the champion racehorse who won the 1952 St. Leger and the Epsom Derby - *Pinza* was a true thoroughbred, clocking up three million miles of main line service between 1961 and 1981, including many visits to Bradford. The locomotive spent the majority of its career based at London's Finsbury Park shed from where it was withdrawn on 31 December 1981. It was scrapped at BR's Doncaster Works in August 1982 – a sad and ignominious end for a magnificent machine. In July 1978, the author of this caption named his cat *Pinza* in honour of the locomotive. The cat went on to outlive the Deltic by 12 years! In the distance on the right, a Class 03 shunter marshals the stock which would form the late evening Bradford to London King's Cross parcels service and, in the adjacent platform, a Metro-Cammell Class 101 DMU can be seen awaiting its next duty. *(John S. Whiteley)*

The Italianate clock tower of Bradford City Hall peers out over the vast expanse of steel and glass forming the roof of the Interchange Bus Station, which opened on Sunday 27 March 1977 - two years later than originally planned and well over budget. The Bradford Transport Interchange development occupied eight acres and consolidated a number of outlying bus depots into a cavernous underground garage for the servicing and maintenance of all locally-based vehicles operated under the West Yorkshire Passenger Transport Executive's 'Metro' banner. Class 08 shunter No. 08224 moves off with a short trip working made up of five empty mineral wagons and two BR standard 20-ton brake vans on 29 March 1978, having been held for a while in the engine release siding, pending the arrival of a London to Bradford passenger train which can be seen unloading in Platform 1. 08224, which will be seen later in this book in its former guise as D3294, had been transferred to Hammerton Street in 1971 and was one of only three locally-based Class 08s at this time. Another 11 arrived later in the year following closure of Leeds Holbeck as a diesel maintenance depot. The former Broomfield coal yard to the left of the locomotive closed in 1976 and had become a somewhat rudimentary car park. *(Peter Fitton)*

Looking quite smart in its off-white with blue stripe livery, this 2-car Metropolitan Cammell Class 101 DMU coasts down into Bradford Exchange in 1982. The Driving Trailer Composite car at the leading end is No. 56394, which entered service at Dundee in 1958. It was transferred to Hull in 1969, then to Leeds Neville Hill after refurbishment at Doncaster Works in January 1977. BR found it difficult to keep the new livery acceptably clean so an alternative blue and grey colour scheme was adopted as standard in the late 1970s. Standing just beyond the passing DMU is Class 03 No. 03060 with its match wagon and a BR standard Covered Carriage Truck (CCT). The ensemble is stabled at the end of a line that once ran into the Broomfield coal sidings. 03060 was transferred from Colchester to Bradford in 1977 and spent much of its time as the Bradford Exchange station pilot, sharing the duty with its sister loco, 03371. It was withdrawn in December 1982 after a service life of 23 years and scrapped at Doncaster Works the following summer. Most of the Victorian era mill and warehouse buildings in the background are long gone, along with the more modern ancillary buildings of the Nelson Street Bradford Central Fire Station which opened in 1971 and closed in 2007. *(Robert Anderson)*

On Sunday 16 May 1982, the 1240 Liverpool to Newcastle service, headed by 'Peak' Class 46 diesel No. 46027, was diverted via the Calder Valley and Bradford due to engineering work between Leeds and Huddersfield. Having reversed at Bradford Exchange station, the train is seen climbing towards St. Dunstan's Junction where it would take the Leeds line. This elevated view was captured from the stairs of the Mill Lane Junction signalbox which assumed control of all trains in and out of Bradford Exchange after the opening of the new station in January 1973. 46027 (formerly D164) had been based at Gateshead since 1969 but was no stranger to Bradford, having been a regular visitor during its time as a Leeds Holbeck loco before its transfer to the North East. It would last another 2½ years in service, being withdrawn in November 1984, aged 22. The rake of rusty mineral wagons standing on one of the two truncated sidings would be pressed into service the following day on the 9K02 scrap train from Springmill Street to Laisterdyke – a working which will be covered in detail later in this book. The prominent soot-stained building on the horizon is St. Ann's Roman Catholic Church which, at the time of writing, had found a new use as a warehouse. *(Gavin Morrison)*

The Exchange station name, familiar in Bradford since 1867, disappeared from 16 May 1983 when the Bradford Interchange title was introduced. However, West Yorkshire PTE's local signage was still referring to Bradford Exchange almost three years later! This evocative night scene at Interchange station on 1 September 1983 highlights veteran English Electric Type 4 (Class 40) diesel No. 40004 waiting for loading to be completed before heading out of Platform 4 with a lengthy overnight parcels working, comprising a mix of BR Mark 1 BG (Bogie Gangwayed) vans and GUVs (General Utility Vans). The change in gradient along the platform is noticeable towards the front of the train. Demand for rail-borne parcels services from Bradford remained healthy in the early to mid-1980s but the traffic then began a gradual decline which meant that some trains could be shortened and handed over to less powerful Class 31s. The Class 40s were in their twilight years in 1983, with a large number already withdrawn, and 40004 was 25 years old at the time of this photograph. It entered service in 1958 as D204 and was one of pioneers of the changeover from steam to diesel on East Anglian express services between Norwich and London Liverpool Street. The locomotive lasted a further year and a day before being withdrawn. *(Jan Rapacz)*

An unusual interloper in the shape of a route learning car No. DB975042 stands in the shade of Croft Street Bridge on the engine release road at Bradford Interchange on a warm June day in 1984. Originally numbered W55019, it was one of a class of 20 high-density single car units built by the Gloucester Railway Carriage & Wagon Company and introduced by BR in 1958 for use on branch line services on the Western and London Midland Regions. These units were nicknamed 'Bubble Cars' and designated Class 122 in the TOPS classification scheme. After only 11 years as a passenger-carrying vehicle, W55019 was converted into a route learner in November 1969 and it worked far and wide for many years helping drivers to gain and refresh their route knowledge. It was finally taken into Network Rail Departmental stock before passing into preservation in 2012. Note the pair of diminutive Reliant Robin 3-wheeled motor vehicles parked up alongside the railway 'Bubble Car.' *(Jan Rapacz Collection)*

By the late 1970s, British Rail realised that a long term modernisation plan was needed to upgrade its aging DMU fleet. Refurbishments were approved for many first generation sets to extend their working lives and to buy time for new designs to be developed. BR was particularly keen to explore the viability of the 'railbus' concept as a cheap option for local short-distance routes. The most promising prototype to emerge was a two-car unit using Leyland National bus components. The Class 140 made its debut in 1981 and, although mechanically sound, it was not a comfortable ride and received some negative reaction. BR was undaunted and pressed ahead with a production order for twenty sets from British Leyland. Externally, these differed slightly from the prototype and were designated Class 141. As the units were sponsored by the West Yorkshire PTE, they carried its corporate branding and Verona green and buttermilk bus livery. They later received the revised red and cream 'MetroTrain' colours after refurbishment. The first Class 141 was handed over in September 1983. Set 009, with leading car No. 55530 facing the camera, is seen at Bradford Interchange in its original livery in 1984. After jolting around the local network for 13 years, the 141s quietly faded away and 12 sets were exported for further use in Iran. The unit featured here was initially preserved but has since been scrapped. *(Andrew Rapacz)*

A quick lunchtime snapshot at Bradford Interchange on an overcast 14 September 1989 finds 47417 in Platform 4 on a short parcels train while a Class 156 'Super Sprinter' unit awaits departure for Manchester. The 156s were among the second tranche of more substantial new units to emerge from the 1980s DMU modernization programme. The first of 114 sets appeared in 1988 and they are still in operation today, although their visits to Bradford have become rare since the introduction of the new CAF Class 195 units in 2019. The first serious incident involving a Class 156 occurred at Bradford Interchange on the evening of 8 May 1989 when 156491 collided heavily with the Platform 4 buffer stops. The unit was only three weeks old at the time and had been running in with a Manchester to Leeds service. Nobody was seriously hurt but the DMU was badly damaged and required major repairs before re-entering service. *(Alan Whitaker)*

Bradford's first introduction to the revolutionary high speed diesel train (HST) came on the weekend of 19/20 March 1977 when brand new Western Region set No. 253021 was stabled at Exchange station as part of an exhibition to promote the new Transport Interchange which was to open a week later. The set, which included power cars Nos. W43042/43, created a lot of interest but it would be another year before the 'Inter-City 125' HSTs would enter service on the East Coast Main Line. Backed by a big national marketing campaign, the design was a huge success. With a top operating speed of 125 m.p.h., the HSTs transformed fast inter-city services in many parts of the country and, in doing so, ousted first generation main line diesels from their traditional stamping grounds. Among those to be cast aside by the HSTs were the iconic 100 m.p.h. Deltics – in their day the fastest diesel locomotives in the world. Here, we find HST power car No. 43178, in BR's later InterCity 'Swallow' livery, at Bradford Interchange at 2043 on 23 March 1988 after arrival from London King's Cross. The new 'Swallow' branding, which replaced BR's familiar double arrow logo, was introduced on 1 May 1987 to coincide with the 21st anniversary of the InterCity brand and was intended to 'symbolise grace and speed.' At least that's what it said in the media blurb. *(Alan Whitaker)*

A dwindling number of first generation DMUs continued to eke out their last years alongside their new, modern replacements. Among them were the remaining Class 110s which had been transferred to Leeds Neville Hill when Bradford Hammerton Street - their home depot for many years - closed in May 1984. On the very wet afternoon of 6 April 1989, one of these veterans struggles up the steep gradient from Bradford Interchange towards Mill Lane with the 1719 from Leeds to Todmorden. The unit was one of the last of its type in service and was, according to the photographer, 'on its last legs,' although it had spent the day gamely deputising for a 'Pacer' unit on the intensive Leeds-Bradford-Leeds 'shuttle' services, in spite of gearbox problems. By this time, the once familiar Class 110s had become a much rarer sight in Bradford, having been displaced on the main Calder Valley services by Class 150 'Sprinter' and Classes 155 and 156 'Super Sprinter' trains. They had served the city well but the era of these early 1960s pioneers of dieselisation in Bradford was coming to a close. *(Robert Anderson)*

The Class 155 two-car units were the first 'Super Sprinter' DMUs to emerge, although only the Class 156s carried that branding. The first of 42 sets – built by Leyland Bus at Workington - was introduced in 1987 and all had been delivered by the end of the following year. The BR order for 35 sets was supplemented by a further seven for West Yorkshire PTE which rolled off the production line in the summer of 1988. Although still based on bus body principles, the 155s were carried on bogies which made them far more comfortable than the rudimentary railbuses of Classes 141-144. They also represented an upgrade on their Class 150 'Sprinter' predecessors. Initial teething troubles relating to the door mechanisms led to the PTE units returning to Leyland Bus for rectification in February 1989. They then settled down to give excellent service. In the early 1990s, BR converted its Class 155 sets into single car units which were then designated Class 153 but WYPTE kept its fleet in the original two-car formations, numbered 155341-347. At the time of writing, all seven of these sets were still in service with Northern Trains but were no longer everyday visitors to Bradford, having been replaced by new CAF Class 195 units. In this view, 155343 - resplendent in its WYPTE red and cream livery - is seen approaching Bradford Interchange on 3 July 1990. *(Peter Fitton)*

BR's desire for a high specification DMU for longer distance express services led to the development of the Class 158 in the late 1980s. A total of 182 two-car sets were built at the Derby Works of British Railways Engineering Limited between 1989 and 1992, with the first entering service for ScotRail in 1990. BR's order was for 172 units and a further ten were built for West Yorkshire PTE. These were numbered 158901-10 and were introduced in April and May 1991. The 158s were superior to the earlier 'Sprinter' family of units, with faster, smoother and quieter acceleration and a 90 m.p.h. top speed, compared to the 75 m.p.h. maximum achieved by Classes 150, 155 and 156. They were also fitted with air conditioning, better-sprung bogies and more comfortable seating. Some units were subsequently increased to three-car formations for use on Trans-Pennine services, including the Calder Valley route via Bradford. The Class 158s are now 30 years old but still fulfill a vital front-line role across many parts of the network, although the recent introduction of new third generation types has seen them gradually relegated to more secondary duties in some areas. 158910, seen here, was the last of the WYPTE units to enter service and was only two months old when recorded entering former Great Northern Railway territory on the St. Dunstan's curve with a Blackpool to York service on 10 July 1991. *(Peter Fitton)*

With eight coaches of Whitsuntide Bank Holiday trippers in tow, veteran Class 40 diesel No. 40108 makes a fine spectacle as it thrashes up the gradient towards Bowling Tunnel on the former Lancashire & Yorkshire Railway main line with a special excursion from Bradford to Blackpool on 26 May 1980. Springmill Street - the last rail-served coal depot on the south side of the city - can be seen on the left. The train is about to pass over the long abandoned remnants of the former Great Northern route from Bradford to Halifax and Keighley via Queensbury. 40108 was almost 20 years old at the time of this view, having entered service in November 1960 as D308, but it did not have much time left. It was withdrawn three months later and had been scrapped by the end of the year. *(Peter Fitton)*

A trackside view of a two-car Class 110 DMU belching out an impressive plume of exhaust as it nears Bowling Junction on a service to Manchester Victoria in 1984. The third track, on the left, is the goods-only 'Down Through Siding' from Bowling Junction to Springmill Street coal yard. It had originally extended to the Bridge Street goods yard but was cut back after closure of that depot in 1962. To reduce the risk of runaways on the steep falling gradient, trains of loose-coupled wagons were ordered to stop here to have their brakes pinned down. The large wooden instruction board reminding railway staff of the need to do this is a survivor from a bygone age. A plan to single this section of line as part of a Mill Lane Junction (Bradford) to Milner Royd Junction (Sowerby Bridge) rationalisation scheme emerged in 1983 but, unusually for the time, BR management saw sense and it was never implemented. *(Andrew Rapacz)*

A panoramic view of the same location as seen on the previous page shows the former Leeds, Bradford & Halifax Junction line from Laisterdyke snaking in from the right to join the ex-L&YR line at Bowling Junction, which is being approached by this 3-car Class 110 DMU on its way to Manchester on 29 June 1981. This direct route opened in 1854 and was used by freight, parcels and passenger services that did not need to go into Bradford and could, therefore, avoid a time-consuming and inconvenient reversal. It was built as a double-track main line but was partly singled in 1970 after closure as a 'through' route. The branch remained operational until 1985 to facilitate access to a scrap metal firm's sidings at Laisterdyke. The rear power car of the DMU is in BR's revised blue/grey livery, which began to be applied to this class of unit in 1979. Mixed livery sets were common at this time as vehicles were being refurbished at Doncaster Works to extend their service lives. The building between the two railways beyond the train was part of the once extensive Ripley Dyeworks (latterly part of the Bradford Dyers Association) which had been integral to the development of Bradford's world famous wool textile industry. *(Robert Anderson)*

On the same day as the previous picture, the photographer has swung round to capture a Bradford-bound service from his vantage point on the high bridge carrying New Cross Street over the railway. Another of the ubiquitous Class 110 DMUs has just emerged from Bowling Tunnel and is about to start its careful descent towards Bradford Exchange station. The Bowling branch joining the main line from the left was reduced to a single line between Laisterdyke and Hall Lane in June 1970, with the redundant track being lifted the following year. Traces of the missing track can still be identified from the sleeper impressions in the ballast. Until 1977, movements on and off the branch were controlled by Bowling Junction signalbox but the structure was badly damaged in an arson attack on the night of 5/6 August. Temporary arrangements were put in place until the control of the points and signals previously worked from Bowling Junction were transferred to Mill Lane Junction signalbox with effect from Sunday, 5 August 1979, thereby establishing a long block section from Low Moor to Mill Lane. *(Robert Anderson)*

A close-up view of the Bowling Tunnel northern portal taken from the brake van of the daily trip working between McIntyre's scrap sidings at Laisterdyke and Springmill Street as it waits to come off the Bowling branch on 4 April 1984. Emerging from the depths of the tunnel is Gloucester Railway Carriage & Wagon Co. single route-learning car, No. DB975042, seen earlier on page 29. When the unit has cleared the crossover, the Laisterdyke trip will be flagged over to the 'Down Through Siding' to gain access the yard at Springmill Street. At the time of its completion in 1850, Bowling Tunnel was the longest in the Bradford area at 1,648 yards. It was superseded in 1878 by Queensbury Tunnel on the Great Northern route to Halifax which is 2,501 yards long but has been abandoned since 1956. *(Steve Hall)*

Class 40 No. 40106 achieved a degree of celebrity status when it was repainted in its original green livery, instead of the standard BR blue, in 1978. Its repaint had been long overdue and it was the only member of its class never to carry corporate blue. Having cleared Bowling Tunnel, the 'green machine' is seen here heading towards Low Moor on 17 June 1979 with an excursion from Heckmondwike to Morecambe, organised by a local Working Men's Club. The train had passed through Low Moor in the opposite direction shortly before this photograph was taken en route from Heckmondwike to Bradford Exchange where it reversed before continuing its journey to the West Coast resort. 40106 was one of 20 Class 40s built by English Electric's Robert Stephenson & Hawthorns works at Darlington. It entered service at Crewe in October 1960 and was originally numbered D306. It was withdrawn from BR service on 21 April 1983 and was saved for preservation. At the time of writing, it was owned by the Class 40 Preservation Society and carries the name *Atlantic Conveyer*. *(John S. Whiteley)*

By the time of this view in 1984, Low Moor No. 2 West was the last operational signalbox between Bradford Mill Lane Junction and Halifax. It was built to the standard L&YR specification and opened on 27 November 1893. Originally, it had a 58-lever frame which was reduced to 48 operational levers in 1948. These had been further reduced to 42 by January 1970 when BR commissioned an individual function switch-operated console. The signalbox was then renamed simply 'Low Moor' and its external name boards were modified accordingly. With a couple of track machines for company on the only siding still remaining in situ, the elderly structure still had two more years of service ahead of it. Closure came on 20 July 1986 when the 'absolute block' section from Halifax was extended to Mill Lane Junction. The metal overbridge in the background once spanned the short-lived Great Northern Railway direct line from Pudsey Greenside and Dudley Hill. This closed to passengers during the First World War but goods services continued until 1933. The former GNR goods shed at Low Moor still survives in private commercial use. *(Andrew Rapacz)*

York-based Class 31 No. 31178 moves out of the Permanent Way siding at Low Moor and slowly traverses the crossover to regain the Down line towards Bradford with a loaded ballast train on 4 July 1979. The train comprises five 'Dogfish' 4-wheel ballast hoppers, with three 'Sea Lion' bogie wagons bringing up the rear. The wasteland on the right is the site of Low Moor steam locomotive shed, which closed on 2 October 1967 and was demolished two years later. Part of the site has since taken on a commendable new lease of life as a nature reserve and butterfly habitat. 31178 was one of a class of 260 Type 2 locomotives built by Brush Traction at Loughborough and was new to Hornsey depot in North London as D5599 in March 1960. It went on to clock up 40 years and three months in front-line BR service, working from a variety of depots. It was finally withdrawn in June 2000 and hung around for another three years before it was sent for scrapping. *(Gavin Morrison)*

HRH The Prince of Wales and his entourage had Class 47 haulage on 6 February 1987 when 47585 *County of Cambridgeshire* took them all to Bradford for an official visit. The immaculate locomotive is seen here bringing some colour to an otherwise soulless railway landscape as it heads the Royal Train past Low Moor on its way to Bradford Interchange. Staff at Stratford (London), the locomotive's home shed, had clearly wanted to ensure that their charge looked its best and the pride they had in their work was obvious. In terms of identity, 47585 had a chequered history. It emerged from Brush Traction, Loughborough, as D1779 in October 1964 and was initially allocated to Sheffield Tinsley. It was renumbered to 47184 in February 1974 and then became 47585 in January 1981, five months before being named in a ceremony at Cambridge station. It was withdrawn in March 1992 and placed in store. Then, in January 1994, it was refurbished and reinstated as No. 47757 in which guise it continued in service until final withdrawal in August 2005. This time there was to be no resurrection and it was scrapped the following year. The disused tracks on the left were all that remained of an extensive network of carriage sidings which were situated within a junction of lines to Heckmondwike. *(John S. Whiteley)*

Low Moor station was a victim of the 1960s cost-cutting purge which decimated the national network in the wake of the Beeching Report. It closed in June 1965 and was demolished. Within 15 years, campaigns to restore stations on lines which had survived the axe began to snowball. Among those highlighted was Low Moor which was included for years on a West Yorkshire PTE list of potential new stations. The opening of the £12 million Transperience Transport Museum Centre on former railway land at Low Moor in July 1995 intensified the clamour but the museum was a white elephant and closed in 1997 after losing a fortune. Undeterred, campaigners kept up the pressure and a new £10.8 million Low Moor station was opened on 2 April 2017 - 52 years after closure of its predecessor. Here, 'Pacer' unit No. 144019 calls with a Huddersfield service on 10 May 2017. A total of 23 two-car Class 144s were introduced in 1986-87. Ten sets, including this one, were later increased to three-car formations by adding a centre car. All the 144s were sponsored by WYPTE from new and ran in Metro livery before being repainted into their operator's colours. They were built by British Rail Engineering at Derby, using Walter Alexander bus bodywork on four-wheeled underframes. After almost 35 years in service, the last of these units was withdrawn by Northern Trains in 2020 and two thirds of the fleet has passed into preservation, including 144019. *(Martin Bairstow)*

The quaintly named Bottom Viaduct, between Lightcliffe and Wyke, provides a fine setting for this view of a two-car Class 110 'Calder Valley' DMU heading for Bradford in 1984. The unit is carrying BR's revised blue and grey livery and looks almost toy-like against the majestic 11-arch stone structure. Bottom Viaduct was designed by the renowned Victorian civil engineer John Hawkshaw and built by the Lancashire & Yorkshire Railway Company in 1850 to carry its Halifax to Bradford line over Bottom Hall Beck. It stands 114 feet at its highest point and was one of two major viaducts constructed in this area by the L&YR. The other was Wyke Viaduct on the 'Pickle Bridge' branch to Brighouse via Bailiff Bridge which crossed the nearby Wyke Beck and closed in 1952. The structure straddled the border between Bradford Council's area of responsibility and that of Calderdale. The arches on the Bradford side were demolished in 1987, reportedly due to mining subsidence, but the section over the border in the Calderdale District still stands as an unusual local landmark. *(Andrew Rapacz)*

The forerunner of the familiar and distinctive Class 110 DMUs, which were the mainstay of Calder Valley services from the early 1960s to the mid-1980s, were the BRCW Class 104 units, introduced in 1957. Although they were mainly deployed on local services in the North West, a small number of these units were allocated to Bradford Hammerton Street in 1958. Unlike their successors, they were not given time to become well established and were soon re-allocated after being replaced by other types. However, Manchester-based examples continued to be regular visitors to Bradford until 1987 when many first generation classes were replaced by new 'Sprinter' trains. Having crossed Bottom Viaduct, a two-car Class 104 set is seen here on a service to Preston, not long after the reintroduction of the direct link via Copy Pit in 1984. This was thanks to the National & Provincial Building Society which wanted staff based at its principal administration centres in Preston and Bradford to be able to travel quickly and easily between the two cities. The company sponsored two trains a day, which could also be used by ordinary passengers. These called at Blackburn, Accrington, Rose Grove, Hebden Bridge and Halifax and paved the way for the frequent and well-used daily services between York, Leeds, Bradford and Blackpool which still use the Copy Pit route today. *(Andrew Rapacz)*

Frost clings to vegetation on both sides of St. Dunstan's curve on a bright winter day in January 1979 as an HST in original livery takes the former Great Northern line with the 1255 Bradford Exchange to London King's Cross. By this time, the importance of the St. Dunstan's triangle was long gone. A station on this site had closed in 1952 and the last of its three signalboxes had been decommissioned in December 1972. Thereafter, the ex-L&YR Mill Lane signalbox, which can be seen behind the train, assumed control of the junctions linking the former L&Y and GNR lines in and out of Bradford. The box opened in 1876 and operated using a traditional mechanical lever frame for 97 years until the new Exchange station was fully opened in June 1973. A new switch-based signalling and points console was then installed to replace the old equipment. This gave the box another 45 years of operational life. It closed in October 2018 when its area of control was transferred to the Rail Operating Centre in York. In its late Victorian heyday, St. Dunstan's was an important interchange point for passengers transferring between main line services and branch trains to and from Halifax and Keighley via Queensbury, which had their own separate platforms. The third part of the St. Dunstan's triangle carried an avoiding curve used by freight trains for City Road and the Queensbury line. *(John S. Whiteley)*

Track workers stand clear as 31411 powers the 0925 Bradford Interchange to Scarborough away from Hall Lane bridge on the steep climb towards Hammerton Street Junction on 26 May 1983. This was a regular Class 31 duty at the time. Unlike numerous other first generation diesel classes which succumbed to early withdrawal, the 31s just kept going and it wasn't until the 1990s that mass withdrawals started to make significant inroads into their numbers. 31411 had a very respectable service life of 44 years and 8 months. It was new in March 1961 as D5691 and allocated to Sheffield Darnall. It was renumbered into the TOPS classification system in 1974 and, in 1982, was one of 70 Class 31s fitted with electric train heating equipment for working regional semi-fast passenger services. The proliferation of 'Super Sprinter' DMUs in the late 1980s/early 90s displaced the 31s from these workings and the ETH equipment was removed. The locomotives were then designated into the 31/5 sub-class and 31411 became 31511. It was withdrawn in 2005 and scrapped. *(John S. Whiteley)*

The unusually long, hot summer of 1976 provided excellent opportunities for photographers to get out and about. On 7 July, Gavin Morrison ventured to Bradford to record this fine view of the first of the 22 production Deltics, No. 55022 *Royal Scots Grey* (formerly D9000), powering up the cutting between Usher Street bridge and Wakefield Road Tunnel with the 1155 Bradford Exchange to London King's Cross. With 3,300 horsepower available, the long climb from Exchange station to Laisterdyke was no big deal for a well maintained Deltic running on dry rails - but it still required a bit of muscle as the plumes of exhaust from the locomotive testify. At the time of this view, Deltics had been a familiar sight in Bradford for 15 years but their dominance on principal East Coast main line express workings would be broken by the progressive introduction of the 125 m.p.h. HSTs from May 1978. *Royal Scots Grey* was new to Edinburgh Haymarket shed, where it was based for most of its career, in February 1961 and it went on to clock up 3.25 million miles in service. It received its 55022 TOPS number in April 1974 and was withdrawn on 2 January 1982. It is one of six Deltics now in preservation. *(Gavin Morrison)*

A daytime empty stock movement comprising a pair of 3-car Class 110 DMU sets descends towards St. Dunstan's in June 1983. Workings such as this were intensive - especially in late evening and early morning - as DMUs were ferried from Exchange station then back again after refuelling and maintenance at Hammerton Street diesel depot. The higher level sidings on the right were mainly used to store redundant stock, pending disposal. A withdrawn Class 08 shunter, No. 08197, can be identified among the DMU cars. This locomotive was never officially allocated to Hammerton Street but was sent there for storage after withdrawal from York in 1982 and remained for almost a year. The other Class 08, to which it is coupled, is very probably 08548 as the pair were noted stored together for several months from April 1983. The latter had been on Hammerton Street's books since September 1975 but was taken out of service in December 1982. Both shunters were sent to Doncaster Works for scrapping during Autumn 1983. The old perimeter retaining walls between Hammerton Street depot and the main line appear to have been recently re-pointed. *(Steve Hall)*

Another of the many historic buildings which were lost to Bradford between the 1950s and 70s was the train shed of the original Leeds, Bradford & Halifax Junction Railway passenger station at Adolphus Street. This imposing building, which loomed over Wakefield Road, featured a succession of elegant spandrels and iron girders forming semi-circular arches which supported a magnificent glazed roof of 104 ft. span. The station opened in 1854 but its location outside the city centre was inconvenient to passengers. Having taken over the LB&HJR, the Great Northern Railway Company secured Parliamentary permission to build a line to a junction with the L&YR main line at St. Dunstan's. This enabled GNR trains to share the L&YR terminus station at Drake Street from 1867. Meanwhile, Adolphus Street station was converted to become the GNR's principal Bradford area goods depot. The remains of the last section of the 1854 train shed were recorded for posterity in December 1970 by photographer Robert Anderson, one of very few people who seemed interested in its fate. Some of the sidings on the extensive Adolphus Street site were still in use at this time but were on borrowed time. By the end of 1971, only a couple of unstaffed Public Delivery Sidings remained open for traffic and these finally succumbed on 1 May 1972. The site was then redeveloped for warehousing.
(Robert Anderson)

A quiet interlude at Hammerton Street Junction in 1977 shows the access into the diesel depot on the left and new warehousing which had obliterated the former Adolphus Street goods depot site on the right. Just visible 'on shed' are a Class 110 DMU and several diesel shunters of Classes 03 and 08. The signalman can be seen keeping an eye on the photographer from the top of the signalbox steps. Opened in 1882, Hammerton Street Junction box had been refitted with a new 75-lever McKenzie & Holland frame in 1957 but was closed on 16 September 1979 when control of all points and signals was transferred to Mill Lane Junction signalbox. Note the miniature outlet signal arms, nearest to the box, which controlled the exit from Loco No. 1 road. The other miniature arms on the left controlled the exit from Loco No. 2 road and the Ballast Sidings. The siding to the right of the main running lines was all that remained of former the Down Goods and associated network of lines providing access to the Adolphus Street yard complex which handled a huge amount of freight from the 1870s to the mid-1960s. By the early post-steam era, it had all but vanished. *(ColourRail)*

Bradford's Bowling steam shed was one of first depots in the country to receive an allocation of diesel railcars. These arrived in 1954 and although the facilities were modified to cater for the new traction, the challenges of trying to maintain diesel units alongside steam locomotives proved difficult and unsatisfactory. As a result, steam was banished to Low Moor in 1958 and the shed was modernized to become Hammerton Street diesel depot – a transformation which took several years to complete. As well as early classes diesel passenger trains, Hammerton Street began to receive an allocation of new Drewry 0-6-0 diesel shunting locomotives in December 1957. These 204 horsepower machines were later designated Class 04 and used mainly as goods depot pilots and for short trip workings. They were joined in 1960 by a batch of BR Class 03s which had the same power rating. Some of these outlasted their predecessors at the depot by more than 10 years. The Class 04s did not survive long enough to carry TOPS numbers and the last of Bradford's contingent was withdrawn in 1970. D2271, seen here just before it was taken out of service, had been a fairly recent addition to the Hammerton Street allocation, arriving from Mirfield in July 1968. It was put into store on 5 October 1969, then withdrawn three weeks later and sold for scrap. However, it escaped into preservation and, at the time of writing, was based on the South Devon Railway. *(Jan Rapacz Collection)*

The most unusual addition to the Hammerton Street depot fleet in the post-steam era was undoubtedly this British Thomson-Houston Class 15 – a type which had been confined to the London area, Hertfordshire and East Anglia and had never worked anywhere near Bradford. As D8237, it had been withdrawn in March 1969 after a main line service life of less than nine years and was then moved to Doncaster Works to be converted into an unpowered carriage heating unit. It was renumbered into BR Departmental stock as DB968002 and arrived in Bradford in July 1969. The former Type 1 spent most of its time heating stock in the Vicar Lane carriage sidings next to Exchange station and had to be dragged up to Hammerton Street for regular maintenance, such as replenishing its water tanks. It is seen here during one such visit in November 1969. Photographs of the unit in its Bradford days are extremely rare - especially in colour - so this image, albeit slightly grainy, is quite a find. DB968002 spent its last months in Bradford stored out of use at Hammerton Street and finally left in September 1971. It then turned up at its former home shed of Finsbury Park in London before embarking on a succession of moves to locations as far afield as Swansea and Colchester. It was finally taken out of Departmental stock in November 1982, then stored until March 1985 when it was taken to a Sheffield scrapyard for disposal. *(Ian Walmsley)*

This September 1969 view at Hammerton Street finds a pair of Class 04 shunters with different cab designs taking a weekend break. Class 04s were frequently paired up cab-to-cab for working in tandem, as seen here. The increased pulling and braking power was especially useful for trip workings on the steeply-graded City Road goods branch and for transfer freights between Adolphus Street and Laisterdyke. D2204 was one of the earliest intake of small diesel shunters which pre-dated BR's 1955 'end of steam' Modernisation Plan. It entered service at West Hartlepool in March 1953 and was transferred to Bradford in September 1967. By the time D2261 arrived new at Hammerton Street in December 1957, the cab design for the Class 04s had been modified, providing a better side view for drivers. D2204 was withdrawn from BR stock a month after this photo was taken but then went on to complete another ten years of service with a private industrial operator. It was scrapped in 1979. D2261, meanwhile, continued in service until March 1970 when it was withdrawn as surplus as there was no work for it. Having been sold to a South Wales scrap dealer, it left Hammerton Street on 3 June 1970 and exacted its revenge by running hot. It had to be detached at Belper, Derbyshire, where it was dumped in a siding for three months before being re-sold and taken by road to Rotherham for scrapping. *(Jan Rapacz Collection)*

A programme of major refurbishment for some classes of first generation DMUs was implemented in the mid-1970s and those so treated started to emerge in a revised, largely off-white livery with a broad blue band. Although much smarter than the boring all-over slab blue which had been applied to replace BR's attractive lined Brunswick green, the new livery was difficult to keep clean and was eventually replaced again by blue and grey. This Class 110 set was the first of its type to receive the mainly off-white variant and is seen here on 12 June 1979, having just arrived back at Hammerton Street. After showing off its pristine new paintwork for the camera, it returned to service. Unfortunately, the identity of the set was not recorded. The Class 110 DMUs were an updated version of the earlier Class 104 and were specifically designed to operate rapidly on steeply-graded lines such as those in the Bradford area. To achieve this high level of performance, each power car had two-180hp Rolls-Royce diesel engines. The first 20 sets were allocated to Hammerton Street from new in 1961, although some were initially based at Darlington for trials on the challenging Stainmore route to Penrith. The final ten sets were sent to Newton Heath depot, Manchester, but were later transferred to join the rest of the fleet at Hammerton Street in an effort to improve maintenance standards. *(Robert Anderson)*

Before it became the depot 'celebrity,' BR Class 03 shunter No. 03371 is seen here taking Sunday off at Hammerton Street on 31 January 1982. With its faded paintwork and its yellow rear buffer beam bizarrely daubed with a patch of unbecoming pale blue, the locomotive was looking rather tired. But all that was about to change with a Works visit due. 03371 had a long on and off association with Bradford which began in September 1968 when it arrived from Cambridge as D2371. It received its new TOPS number in February 1974, while allocated to York, and returned to Hammerton Street in its new guise in July 1976. This shunter was unique in being the only dual braked locomotive in the BR fleet with a conical exhaust. Its main duties during its first 4 ½ years as a Bradford-based locomotive included pilot duties at both Exchange and Forster Square stations – the latter requiring a trip to Leeds to access the former Midland line into Bradford via Shipley. For several years after its return in 1976, 03371 was occasionally out-based at Halifax for shunting the ex-L&YR depot at Shaw Syke and trip workings to Sowerby Bridge. These were longstanding duties for the Hammerton Street Class 03 fleet until December 1980 when goods services at Halifax were withdrawn. *(Alan Whitaker)*

A withdrawn Birmingham Railway Carriage & Wagon Company car from a Class 104 DMU set is robbed for spares at Hammerton Street in June 1983, before being dragged outside to one of the depot's storage sidings to await disposal. This was very probably a Manchester-based car which had turned up for maintenance after working in on a Calder Valley service but was then found to have a serious fault which prompted its premature retirement. Class 104s were the predecessors of the more familiar Class 110 units which had been a feature of the Bradford railway scene since 1961. Window frame corrosion problems which had become evident on the Class 104s early in their careers led to the Class 110s being fitted with alloy frames. However, the most noticeable difference between the two generations of BRCW units were the distinctive high cab windows of the Class 110s – a pleasing design and, aesthetically, an improvement on what had gone before. *(Steve Hall)*

During a visit to Doncaster Works in September/October 1982, 03371 received a full repaint, which included black instead of yellow buffer beams. The locomotive is seen back at home a couple of months later, still waiting for its Hammerton Street allocation stickers to be re-applied. At the time of this view, the depot's other Class 03 - No. 03060 - was about to be withdrawn, leaving 03371 to soldier on as the last of its type at Hammerton Street. It continued its forays down to Bradford Exchange to shunt parcels stock and, when not down there, was used as the depot shunter. The higher level siding occupied by the locomotive was at the end of what, in steam days, had been part of the 'coaling stage road.' *(Alan Whitaker)*

A nicely composed panorama of the north side of Hammerton Street depot, taken from over the perimeter wall, on a quiet evening in June 1983. The proximity of the tightly packed Victorian housing of Leeds Road is well illustrated. The former GNR steam locomotive shed on this site, dating from 1876, had been known as Bowling and coded 37C in early BR days. It was re-coded 56G and re-named Hammerton Street when a new Wakefield Motive Power District was created in 1956 and retained that identity when it was converted to a diesel depot two years later. In 1967, it became 55F which had been the old Manningham steam shed code until closure in April of that year. When traditional depot codes were abolished in May 1973, Hammerton Street became simply 'HS.' Redundant DMU cars can be seen awaiting their fate in the storage sidings on the left. The Class 08 shunter, hemmed in by more DMU stock, was also in store at the time while, in the distance, Bradford's last Class 03, No. 03371, awaits its next duty. The lull in activity on the 'fuelling road' to the right would be short-lived as units would soon be arriving to replenish their tanks at the end of their day's work. After taking on fuel, they would then pass through the carriage washing plant which can be seen in the middle distance. *(Andrew Rapacz)*

The Regional Civil Engineers' inspection saloon - known as the 'York Saloon' - waits to takes fuel at Hammerton Street in July 1983. This distinctive set comprised two former Class 100 Gloucester Railway Carriage & Wagon Company 'semi-lightweight' cars which had been taken into Departmental stock in May 1974. The car facing the camera is DB975539 (formerly E56101) with DB975346 (formerly E51116) coupled behind. Both of these vehicles had been withdrawn from front-line service at Norwich depot in October 1972 and were held in safe storage until they were transferred into the Departmental pool, although they were not initially paired together. The York Saloon was a familiar sight at Hammerton Street where it was based from 1981 until the depot's closure in 1984. It was then transferred to Leeds Neville Hill, along with all the other Bradford units. It continued in Departmental use throughout the Eastern Region until 1993 when it was finally withdrawn. A total of 40 Class 100 sets were built in 1957-58, but none were ever allocated to Hammerton Street while in capital stock. *(Steve Hall)*

A few days before leaving Hammerton Street to see out its final years in the North East, 03371 was still being put to good use as the depot shunter. It is seen here dragging Class 110 DMU Motor Composite car No. 51846 from the repair shop. By then, the '03' had become something of a local celebrity, with enthusiasts from far and wide making special trips to see it. 03371 finally left Hammerton Street at the end of July 1983 after a total of eleven and a half years based at the depot. Having first arrived in September 1968, it was transferred away in March 1973 but returned in 1976 for another seven-year stint. The departure of 03371 left Bradford without a Class 03 for the first time since 1960. The locomotive ended its career with four years at Gateshead and was finally withdrawn in November 1987. It then passed into preservation. *(Steve Hall)*

Main line diesels were never frequent visitors to Hammerton Street, which was a dedicated DMU and shunter depot, although they did appear from time to time in connection with stock moves. On 8 March 1984, Thornaby's Class 31, No. 31282, was rostered to collect withdrawn DMU vehicles and can be seen here waiting for 08497 to move away from two Class 110 centre cars it has just shunted on to one of the storage sidings. The '31' would then couple up and take them away. The other sidings were usually full of stored stock but it seems that there had been a concerted effort to start clearing the decks in the run-up to the depot's closure and the lines were surprisingly empty. The Class 08 occupying the elevated siding is 08503, one of 11 transferred from Leeds Holbeck after its closure as a maintenance facility in October 1978. Until then, Hammerton Street had never had a large allocation of Class 08s. The first two to arrive in the early 1970s soon replaced the less powerful Class 03s on some of their long-established local duties. These included regular workings to Armley Moor and Stanningley and the City Road to Laisterdyke trips. The smaller shunters continued to be the preferred motive power for the out-based Halifax duties, referred to earlier, but engineering works trains at Halifax in the early 1980s employed Class 08s. *(Steve Hall)*

Driver Frank Bastow eases a 3-car Class 110 set out of the Hammerton Street running shed on the evening of Sunday 22 April 1984. The leading car is Motor Brake Composite No. 51810, with centre car 59812 and 51846 making up the formation, but out of view. With three weeks to go before closure, the quiet efficiency of the depot's weekend operations continued as normal but there was a shadow hanging over the place and it was a difficult time for staff. Some of the older men who were in a position to take early retirement did so, but the rest of the workforce had to accept transfer to Leeds, apply for vacancies elsewhere or seek redundancy and leave the industry. *(Alan Whitaker)*

It is Sunday, 6 May 1984 – a week before closure – and Hammerton Street already exudes an air of something about to be lost. An off-duty Class 110 DMU can be seen poking out of the running shed, with a sister unit and a Metro-Cammell further back. From the left are the heavy maintenance shed, the running shed and the former steam locomotive repair shop, dating from GNR days. This building was equipped with an overhead crane and a drop-pit which enabled the depot to maintain and repair its fleet of DMUs and shunters and replace engines and other equipment, if required. Defective units from other depots were also attended to if the need arose. The influx of Class 08s from Leeds Holbeck in October 1978, referred to on Page 64, led to Hammerton Street's allocation of diesel shunters spiralling from six to seventeen, with a consequent increase in its maintenance workload and operational responsibilities. Additional duties which then fell to Bradford included the provision of pilot locos for Leeds City station. However, by the time of closure, there were only seven Class 08s left on the books. *(Alan Whitaker)*

The running shed at Hammerton Street had been roofless since steam days and there was also a big hole in the back wall due to a shunting mishap. Repairs were not deemed to be necessary by the railway hierarchy as the building was otherwise sound and it continued to be used to stable units right to the end. With just seven days of service left, the running shed hosted several Class 110 sets. The set nearest to the camera comprised 51842, 59709 and 51813, with car 51838 just visible on the adjacent line. This was coupled to 51816, which is out of view. BR's announcement that Hammerton Street depot was to be closed was made on 28 July 1983, with May 1984 given as the target date. Planning began immediately to facilitate the transfer of all operational activities and most of the staff to Leeds Neville Hill. So, within 30 years, Bradford Hammerton Street went from being one of the country's pioneering diesel depots with a reputation for high maintenance standards to redundancy and oblivion. *(Alan Whitaker)*

On the same day as the previous picture, Metro-Cammell Class 101 twin-set 51433 and 51499 stand over one of the illuminated inspection pits in the maintenance shed. Ten weeks earlier, this set had been chartered by the National Union of Railwaymen to operate a 'Protest Special' up the Settle & Carlisle line which was under threat of closure. Among the guests on board was the Deputy Leader of the Labour Party, Roy Hattersley MP, who supported retention of route and was among a number of high-profile opposition MPs who put pressure on Margaret Thatcher's Conservative Government to reject BR's closure plans. The ill-founded case for closure unravelled under the challenges and scrutiny of thousands of well-organized objectors the line was saved in 1989. The Class 110 car at the far end of the shed on the left is 51830. *(Alan Whitaker)*

The Gloucester Railway Carriage & Wagon Company single car route learning unit, DB975042, seen on earlier pages, takes a bath in the Hammerton Street washer during the last week of operations at the depot in May 1984. The plant was installed when Hammerton Street became a diesel depot in 1958 and was part of the routine maintenance regime. Units which needed fuelling first had to pass through the inspection building, seen here on the left, before proceeding on to the fuelling point, which had five separate dispensers. They then exited via the washer. *(Steve Hall)*

With the clock ticking down on railway operations Hammerton Street, Shed Master Granville Dobson is seen at work in his office on Sunday, 6 May 1984. He would take up another management position at Leeds when the depot closed a week later. Granville Dobson was a dyed-in-the-wool Bradford railwayman, with long experience in the Operating Department. He had previously worked as a steam locomotive fireman, based at Low Moor shed, before eventually rising through the management ranks. In only a few days, the office would be cleared and the potted plants on the windowsill would need to find a new home. The diesel shunter standing outside in the shed yard is 08239, a relatively recent addition to the Hammerton Street ranks which had arrived at the end of 1982. *(Alan Whitaker)*

Only three days to go before closure and the running shed at Hammerton Street is empty, apart from this unidentified single Class 110 power car which was dumped on its own at the back. The date is Thursday, 10 May 1984 and the photographer recalls that the whole depot seemed eerily silent. It was clear that the transition to Leeds Neville Hill was already well underway. *(Alan Whitaker)*

Bradford's last local trip working was a daily train of scrap metal from McIntyre's siding at Laisterdyke to Springmill Street yard, just off Manchester Road – reporting number 9K02. This was the only train still using the line between Bowling Junction and Laisterdyke via Hall Lane, part of which can be seen crossing Mount Street bridge in the background. On 11 May 1984, and with closure of Hammerton Street depot just two days away, 08239 heads the very last 9K02 trip down to Springmill Street. There, it would collect empty wagons to take up to Laisterdyke in exchange for a rake loaded by McIntyre's staff. The loaded wagons would then be returned to Springmill Street to await onward transit to their final destination using a main line diesel locomotive sent from Healey Mills, near Wakefield. From Monday, 14 May, Healey Mills would be responsible for dealing with the McIntyre's traffic which would see daily forays along the Bowling branch by main line locomotives for the first time in years. Class 31s were the usual motive power rostered for this duty. *(Steve Hall)*

Thirty years after the publicity fanfare and back-slapping that accompanied the arrival of Bradford's first modern diesel railcar, this defective Class 110 set was the only occupant of Hammerton Street depot on the last afternoon – Sunday, 13 May 1984. The last booked DMU departure had been a few hours earlier at 1150 a.m. but the depot did not officially close until one minute after midnight, bringing down the curtain on 108 years of motive power history on the site. The two cars seen here – 51827 and 51829 – had been based at Hammerton Street since new in 1962 and were the last to leave. Having been left inside the redundant repair shed for a few days, they were finally moved to Leeds Neville Hill. *(Alan Whitaker)*

A year after closure, the maintenance shed at Hammerton Street was revived to provide safe storage for various preserved railway stock. An early occupant was a Class 506 'Hadfield' electric multiple unit, purchased for the ill-fated Low Moor Transport Museum. A surprising new arrival on 24 October 1988 was Class 77 EM2 No. 27000 *Electra* which had been repatriated to the UK for preservation after 15 years with Netherlands State Railways. The locomotive was one of seven of its type built in 1953-54 to haul express passenger services on the newly electrified Sheffield to Manchester via Woodhead route. The Class 77s were all withdrawn in 1968 and sold for use on the Dutch railway system where they entered service in 1970-71. One was broken up for spares but the other six worked until June 1986. *Electra* was one of two of its class repatriated to the UK and a third entered preservation in Holland. Having been repainted from Dutch livery into BR green, it is seen here being shunted into the shed by 47144, in Railfreight Distribution colours. 27000 did not stay long in Bradford. It left Hammerton Street in May 1989, with the other preserved stock departing over the following months. The abandoned depot was then left to await its fate and the whole site was cleared in 1991 to make way for a bus garage. *(Robert Anderson)*

The same location as the cover picture, but two years earlier, as an unidentified Class 47 climbs towards Laisterdyke with the lunchtime service to London King's Cross in January 1975. The industrial landscape in the foreground, which had typified this part of Bradford since the early 19th century, contrasts with the modern buildings of the city centre beyond. Notable among the recent developments in the middle distance are the sprawling warehouses built on the site of the Adolphus Street goods depot which, only 20 years earlier, was still one of the busiest railway yards in the whole of BR's West Riding District. The vehicle scrapyard on the left was a well-known 'landmark' for regular passers-by and the Bedford van on top of the pile was still there 2 ½ years later, as the cover picture testifies. *(John S. Whiteley)*

The transition from steam to diesel operation in the West Riding picked up pace during 1967 and an influx of Class 24 and 25 Type 2s arrived at Leeds Holbeck to take over some local passenger services, including the Bradford and Harrogate portions of London expresses which they worked to and from Leeds. The first to arrive were sometimes paired up with steam locomotives on Bradford-Leeds portions but closure of the last remaining West Riding steam sheds on the weekend on 30 September/1 October 1967 put an end to such arrangements. More Type 2s were then transferred to Leeds and they became an everyday sight at Bradford Exchange. However, by the time of this view on 10 May 1971, all the Holbeck Class 24s had been earmarked for transfer to Scotland. The first three left in July with the rest following in October. D5098, seen here climbing towards Laisterdyke on the Bradford portion of a London King's Cross service, was one of the last to leave and arrived at its new home still carrying its obsolete BR green livery. Along with several other former Holbeck Class 24s which went North of the border, this locomotive was declared surplus by the Scottish Region in August 1975 was put into store in serviceable condition - but it never worked again and was cut up in 1976. *(Robert Anderson)*

It is now 1980 and HSTs had become established as the regular motive power for principal Bradford to London services, having ousted the Deltics. Class 47s also appeared on London trains at this time but these tended to operate the slower services which had more stops further south. From a similar vantage point to the photograph on the previous page, an HST in original livery glides effortlessly towards Laisterdyke with the 1115 Bradford Exchange to King's Cross on 3 October 1980. The two tracks on the left formed a locomotive run round loop on the line to Bowling Junction which was brought into use in 1979 to improve shunting operations for the McIntyre's scrap traffic. *(John S. Whiteley)*

The second tranche of production 'Pacer' units were the Class 142s. A total of 96 two-car sets were built in 1985-87 by Leyland Bus and BREL, making them the most numerous Pacer trains on the network. Although they were an improvement on their Class 141 predecessors and gave 35 years of cheap and mainly reliable service, they were no more popular, even after improvements in the 1990s. Their 'cattle trucks' reputation was fuelled by negative media coverage as they continued to be used on services which clearly needed more capacity, especially at peak times. The 142s were based on a wider version of the Leyland National bus body which provided 121 seats in each set but they were hopelessly inadequate on some of the routes they were called on to operate. Here, we see 142004, adorned in Greater Manchester PTE livery, climbing towards Laisterdyke on a service to Leeds on 24 October 1988. This unit made history on Friday 27 November 2020 when it was last Northern Pacer train to run in service. After arrival at Manchester Victoria from Kirby, it was sent empty to Newton Heath depot and was immediately 'retired.' Because of the Covid-19 pandemic lockdowns, the end of the Pacer era went largely unnoticed. A few railway staff displayed a small commemorative banner on the platform at Manchester Victoria as 142004 prepared to head off to the depot - and that was it. *(Robert Anderson)*

47443 *North Eastern*, in BR 'large logo' livery, passes the Laisterdyke station site with a short train of parcels vans from Leeds on 6 April 1992. These regular workings had been a feature of local railway operations for many years but the traffic was dwindling and loadings were much lighter than they had been at the start of the 1980s. This Class 47 had started life as D1559 in March 1964, based at Sheffield Tinsley. It was renumbered into the TOPS series ten years later and named in May 1988. Withdrawal came in October 1993 and the locomotive was scrapped in 1996. The former GNR station at Laisterdyke closed on 4 July 1966 and was demolished in 1968. Only eight years later, consultants were already recommending that a new station should be considered. Their 1976 report to the West Yorkshire PTE also suggested that Bramley and Armley Moor should be restored to the network. These intermediate stations between Bradford Exchange and Leeds had closed on the same day as Laisterdyke. A new station to serve Bramley opened on 12 September 1983 but Laisterdyke and Armley are still waiting for something to happen. Whether it ever will is debatable. *(John S. Whiteley)*

For more than a century until the mid-1960s, Laisterdyke had been a major rail hub where four routes converged and separate goods yards handled huge tonnages of local freight. It was also a transhipment point where goods wagons for locations further afield were marshalled, then sent on their way. But, by the time of this view on 29 June 1972, business in the last operational yard at Laisterdyke was much diminished. Class 08 No. D3294 is arriving with a trip freight from City Road, comprising a Continental Ferryvan, one wagon of scrap and three empty mineral wagons. This was a typical load in 1972 but the traffic would be soon handed over to road transport with closure of City Road yard two months later. Laisterdyke yard would follow suit by the end of the decade, closing on 3 August 1979. The single line curving away on the right was still used by a daily freight to Dudley Hill. This had been the main line to Wakefield which closed to passengers in 1966 and to freight beyond Dudley Hill in February 1968. The remaining stub from Laisterdyke East Junction was then singled. Also deviating at East Junction was the last remnant of the former GNR line to Shipley via Idle. This short section was retained until the summer of 1973 to provide access to the English Electric Company's foundry siding which branched off at Dick Lane. *(Stuart Baker)*

80

Quarry Gap yard at Laisterdyke had been another important collection and distribution point for goods traffic on the former Great Northern network in the Bradford area. It closed on 7 October 1968 but some heavily overgrown sidings remained for a while afterwards. One of them is seen here on 29 June 1972 being occupied by the burned-out shell of Hammerton-Street based Class 110 DMU power car No. 52074 which had caught fire at Bescar Lane, Lancashire, while working a Sunday service from Southport to Manchester on 9 May 1971. The fire was caused by an electrical fault and spread quickly to the adjoining centre trailer car, No. 59705, which was also badly damaged. The power car at the other end of the set was detached and saved from the inferno. Thanks to the swift actions of the crew – and an off-duty driver who was travelling as a passenger on the train - there were no fatalities or injuries. The severely damaged cars were returned to Bradford and, after a year languishing at Hammerton Street, they were dragged up to Quarry Gap for disposal. The remnants of scrap metal in the foreground are what remained of the centre car, No. 59705. Class 110 DMUs had a long history of fires, usually caused by exhaust system faults, but the severity of Bescar Lane incident was much more serious than any previous occurrences. *(Stuart Baker)*

With the exertion of the relentless climb from Exchange station now behind it, ETH-fitted 31406 has breached the summit and begins the less taxing run on the falling gradient towards Leeds on the 0925 Bradford to Scarborough on 8 February 1983. The six-coach train has just passed the redundant Laisterdyke East Junction signalbox which had been replaced by a ground frame in July 1970. The ground frame lasted only nine years before being abolished and the Dudley Hill line was then operated as a long siding until its closure in 1981. With its passenger station, goods yards and junctions now gone, Laisterdyke's role as one of the most important railway hubs in the area was becoming a distant memory. *(John S. Whiteley)*

The first purpose-built Park-and-Ride commuter station in the country was New Pudsey which opened on 6 March 1967. The station, just off the Leeds Ring Road, was built specifically for motorists in an effort to ease traffic congestion in both Bradford and Leeds. The town of Pudsey, just over a mile away, had lost both its stations in 1964 but New Pudsey was not intended as a replacement, although it did offer the locals the option of either driving or walking to catch a train. Similarly, it proved popular for residents of Farsley, which was slightly closer to the station than Pudsey. On 6 March 1987 - the 20th anniversary of the opening of New Pudsey - a two-car Class 150/2 Sprinter DMU set, No. 150226, calls with a service from Manchester Victoria to Leeds via Bradford. The unit is in as-built condition before the addition of yellow ends. Unlike the earlier Class 150/1 Sprinters, the second batch of 85 units, introduced in 1987, were designed with front end gangway connections so they could provide through passenger access when working in tandem and with the later 'Super Sprinters.' Although they are becoming a bit long in the tooth, the Class 150s have proved sturdy and reliable and are still operating on the West Yorkshire network. *(Martin Bairstow)*

Back at Laisterdyke on 24 March 1977 and 08548 waits to depart from East Junction with a single wagon load of girders for steel stockholders, Henry Barrett & Sons Ltd. who had their own private siding at Dudley Hill. This was to become the only traffic on the branch after closure of Dudley Hill goods yard on 17 December 1979. The yard had been reduced to an unstaffed Public Delivery Siding from 13 September 1965 but traffic remained buoyant until the mid-1970s when it began to fall into terminal decline. However, the Barrett traffic was still sufficient to justify keeping the line from Laisterdyke open for a couple more years after closure of Dudley Hill PDS. *(Steve Hall)*

Having arrived at Dudley Hill, this view from the cab of 08548 shows that the brake van has been detached in preparation for shunting the loaded wagon on to Barrett's siding, which branched off what had been the Down Wakefield to Bradford main line. This traffic continued until 7 September 1981 when the Laisterdyke to Dudley Hill line officially closed. It had been a long and slow decline for the former main line which had begun in 1952 with the closure of Dudley Hill passenger station. The last of the intermediate stations closed in 1964 and direct passenger services between Bradford and Wakefield finally ended in 1966. *(Steve Hall)*

Although it had been a major player in the disposal of BR steam locomotives in the 1960s, scrap dealer Arnott Young's yard at Dudley Hill tended to go under the radar. The firm cut up many locomotives in its yards in the Midlands, South Yorkshire, the North East and Scotland but the Bradford operation mainly dealt with general heavy scrap and only a few engines met their end at Dudley Hill. However, in the winter of 1976, word got around that something interesting had turned up - and this was it. 02001 was one of twenty small diesel hydraulic shunters built by the Yorkshire Engine Company, of Sheffield, in 1960-61. These 170 horsepower short wheelbase shunters were designed for use in restricted areas, such as docks, and on sidings with tight curves. They spent their short working lives in the Liverpool, Manchester and Preston areas and until 02001 appeared, none of the class had ever been to Bradford. So, for a few weeks in February/March 1976, this little engine caused quite a stir. 02001 began life as D2851 in 1960 and was one of only three of its type to survive long enough to carry a Class 02 TOPS number. It was withdrawn from Allerton (Liverpool) shed in June 1975, still carrying its original BR green livery, and sold for scrap. This view dates from 4 March 1976 - a week before cutting began. By 18 March, there was no trace of it. *(John Holroyd)*

Diesel shunters from Hammerton Street shed started to appear at City Road goods depot on pilot duties in the early 1960s - well before the end of steam traction. For the first few years, only one single 204 horsepower Class 03 or 04 was required to shunt the yard, with main line steam locomotives working the heavy inward and outward traffic on the steeply graded 1 ¼ -mile branch line from Horton Junction on the Bradford to Thornton route. However, when steam disappeared with closure of Low Moor shed at the beginning of October 1967, the shunters were often paired up to increase haulage capacity and braking power. This continued for a few years until Hammerton Street received an allocation of the more powerful 350 horsepower Class 08s. One of these was D3294 which arrived from Royston in March 1971 and was only the second of its type allocated to the depot at that time – the first being D3547 which had arrived a few months earlier. It is seen here making up its train which, unusually, included a rail-borne crane. The City Road branch continued to be rail served for seven years after closure of the Thornton line to all traffic in June 1965 but by the time of this view in July 1972, BR had already announced its intention to cease operations. *(Clive Weston)*

Hammerton Street's other early 1970s Class 08, D3547, shunts the City Road coal drops on 14 July 1972 – two weeks before the yard had been due to close. BR had announced 31 July as the closure date but implementation was deferred for a month. The yard finally closed on 28 August 1972, four years short of its centenary. City Road had been one of Bradford's most important goods depots. Opened in 1876, it was built to serve the prosperous industrial district around Thornton Road which had seen rapid expansion in the mid-19th century. The yard had an extensive network of sidings which handled freight to and from destinations all over the country. It was so busy that it had its own signalbox until the 1920s. Traffic remained heavy until the 1960s when decline set in as BR lost more and more business to road hauliers. City Road was downgraded to an unstaffed Public Delivery Siding on 5 June 1967 but it continued to generate steady revenue for BR. Its main customers were coal merchants, a scrap metal dealer and a firm of international freight forwarders which occupied the former GNR goods warehouse. This regular traffic was evidently not enough to save it and City Road became yet another victim of BR accountants. As for D3547, it was repainted into BR corporate blue at Doncaster Works in March 1973 and renumbered 08432. It remained a Hammerton Street loco until its withdrawal ten years later. *(Gerald Baxter)*

Apart from the City Road branch, the only other rail facility to survive closure of the Bradford-Thornton line was Horton Park coal yard. The neighbouring yard at Great Horton had closed, along with Thornton, in June 1965 and some of its business had been transferred to Horton Park. Astonishingly for the time, BR approved modest investment at Horton Park to facilitate the additional business from several coal merchants who had been Great Horton customers for many years. This included the installation of new coal hoppers and provision of more stacking space. To minimise maintenance costs, the yard's original seven sidings were reduced to two to create what the BR Commercial Department would have regarded as a 'streamlined operation.' In practice, it was anything but streamlined as operations were often interrupted by derailments caused by poor track condition. This head-on view from the entrance to Horton Park yard on 29 June 1972 shows D3294 – a regular visitor in the last weeks of operation – shunting wagons in the overgrown sidings. The severed connection to some of the sidings removed in 1965 can be seen in the foreground. *(Stuart Baker)*

After visiting Horton Park, photographer Stuart Baker cycled to St. Dunstan's to record another view of the City Road branch freight on 29 June 1972. The train has just emerged from St. Dunstan's Tunnel on the former Bradford & Thornton Railway and crossed over to join the Bradford to Leeds main line. The exhaust being emitted from D3294 shows it is working hard to pick up speed on the 1 in 50 rising gradient to Laisterdyke where its load would be sorted for onward transit. The last vehicle before the brakevan is a Continental Ferryvan laden with goods from the international freight forwarding company at City Road, referred to on page 87. Although the line from St. Dunstan's to Horton Junction and City Road was very rarely visited by main line diesels, it was occasionally used to test the pulling and braking power of new types on steep gradients. Among those reported to have been tested on the branch was a Clayton Type 1 (Class 17) No. D8501 which was involved in various trials while temporarily allocated to Ardsley during September/early October 1963. The locomotive is also said to have been tested between Laisterdyke and Shipley via Idle, another steeply-graded local branch. It obviously did not impress and returned to its home shed in Glasgow, never to be seen in Bradford again. Unfortunately, no photographic evidence of any of those tests has so far emerged. *(Stuart Baker)*

The first major railway closure in the Bradford area in the post-steam era was the Shipley (Windhill) to Idle goods line. Until 1964, it had been part of the former GNR through route from Laisterdyke which connected with the ex-Midland main line at Shipley. Apart from a short stub to serve a private siding near Laisterdyke, the section beyond Idle closed on 2 November 1964. This meant the end of goods services at Eccleshill but the yards at Idle and Windhill were retained. Responsibility for providing locomotives and crews for the remaining branch operations then transferred from Low Moor to Manningham. The line was steam-operated until closure of Manningham shed on 29 April 1967, after which it became a Leeds Holbeck diesel duty.

BR Sulzer Type 2s of Classes 24 and 25 were the regular traction but the diesel era on the Idle branch was destined to be short-lived. The line closed on 7 October 1968. With just five weeks to go before withdrawal of these services, Class 25 No. D7568 starts the climb from Windhill with 7P40 - the morning trip from Bradford Valley Road to Idle - on 30 August 1968. Its payload amounted to just one wagon of coal - hardly taxing for a 1,250 horsepower locomotive and hopelessly uneconomic. In the background, the Leeds to Shipley main line can be seen being joined by the branch from Ilkley just before Guiseley Junction signalbox. *(David Peel)*

A few weeks before the view on the previous page, Holbeck's Class 24, No. D5113, descends towards Windhill with empties from Idle to Bradford Valley Road. These included a wooden-bodied ventilated van which is evidence that Idle yard was still handling more than just coal traffic, even at this late stage in its existence. D5113 was the last of its type built without a roof-mounted four-digit train reporting number headcode box. Instead, the first 114 Class 24s carried old-fashioned front-end marker lights with white background discs to indicate the type of train being operated. This locomotive had been among a tranche of BR Sulzer Type 2s transferred to Leeds Holbeck in 1967 to take over former steam duties. It stayed until October 1971 when it was sent to Scotland to see out the rest of its ridiculously short career of less than 15 years, which ended in 1975. It was scrapped in 1977. *(David Peel)*

Thackley was the only station on the Laisterdyke to Windhill line without a goods yard. Substantial facilities, including a warehouse, loading docks and rail weighbridges, were provided at both Ecclesfield and Idle but Thackley's one-platform passenger halt did not open for business until 1878 - three years after the other stations. The passenger service was axed in 1931 and freight became the mainstay of the line, providing an important and heavily-used direct link between the North and Skipton, the Laisterdyke transhipment yards and the big marshalling yards at Ardsley and Wrenthorpe, near Wakefield. A large amount of local goods traffic was also generated, with both Windhill and Idle yards being particularly busy until well into the 1960s. All that was in the past by the time of this view of an unidentified Class 25 passing Thackley on its way to Idle on 22 August 1968. The remains of the station platform are just visible behind the train. *(David Peel)*

Idle yard on 6 June 1968 finds Class 25 D7624 in charge of shunting operations. The yard appears to contain a respectable number of wagons, demonstrating that the featherweight load seen on page 91 was not necessarily typical in the last months of services on the line. The sturdy former Great Northern Railway goods warehouse, with its separate canopies over the loading bay doors, appears to be in surprisingly excellent condition at a time when railway buildings on secondary lines with a limited lifespan were being left to decay. D7624 was one of the later batches of Class 25s to emerge in the attractive two-tone BR green livery and with deeper front cab windows. A total of 327 of these versatile Type 2s were built between 1961 and 1967, mostly at BR's Derby and Darlington Works, but the construction of some – including D7624 – were sub-contracted to Beyer Peacock Ltd. of Manchester. It was new into service in July 1965 at Sheffield Tinsley but was a Leeds Holbeck loco at the time of this view. It left Holbeck in 1970 for five years on the Western Region, based variously at Newport, Plymouth and Bristol. In 1974, it received its 25274 TOPS number and, a year later, moved to Bescot where it spent its last seven years before withdrawal in May 1982. It was scrapped at Swindon Works in 1985. *(David Peel)*

Springmill Street was the last railway goods yard on the south side of Bradford to survive BR's cost-cutting closures of the 1960s and 70s. This former Lancashire & Yorkshire yard, off Manchester Road, opened in 1868 and, throughout its history, was principally a coal depot with an extensive network of sidings, including two serving a bank of 26 double coal drops. But by the time of this view on 26 April 1984, its only purpose was to deal with trains of scrap from Laisterdyke firm, J. McIntyre, which had a large breakers yard and metal recycling business at Planetrees Road. Dwarfed by the high-rise flats of Manchester Road, 08517 takes a rest after working the daily 9K02 trip to McIntyre's. This involved propelling empty wagons to Bowling Junction where the train would cross over before reversing up the Bowling branch to reach its destination at Laisterdyke. It would then return with loaded wagons which were left at Springmill Street to await collection by a main line locomotive for onward transit to Healey Mills marshalling yard near Wakefield. From there, they would then be tripped to their final destination which, at this time, was a steelworks near Rotherham. *(Alan Whitaker)*

Another view of 08517 at Springmill Street on 26 April 1984, this time framed between two coal hoppers. The coal yard had closed to rail traffic in November 1983 but was still being used by local merchants, one of whose lorries van be seen on the far right. The locally-worked McIntyre's scrap trains using a Hammerton Street Class 08 ended on Friday, 11 May 1984 and the yard closed completely on 7 July. Thereafter, the Laisterdyke trains travelled directly from Healey Mills and continued to use the Bowling branch until September 1985. They were then re-routed away after installation of a new direct connection with McIntyre's siding from the main Leeds-Bradford line.

The previous main line connection had been removed in 1970, leaving the scrap siding accessible only from Bowling Junction. Track-lifting at Springmill Street goods yard began soon after closure and the site was eventually sold. It then became a go-kart track and, in more recent times, a tyre dump which was destroyed by fire in November 2020, releasing a huge pall of acrid black smoke across the district and triggering closure of the Bradford to Halifax main line for several days. November 2020 also saw the start of demolition of the landmark Manchester Road tower blocks to make way for new housing. *(Alan Whitaker)*

Repainting of the BR diesel fleet into the new corporate blue livery began in the last quarter of 1966 but, with several thousand locomotives to deal with, it was well into the 1980s before the job was completed. Still carrying its original green livery, D3294 draws the daily McIntyre's trip from Springmill Street to Laisterdyke over Hall Lane level crossing on 15 November 1973. The old wooden crossing gates had been replaced in October 1968 by electrically-operated lifting barriers and road warning lights controlled from the signalbox. D3294 received its 08224 TOPS number in February 1974, along with several other Hammerton Street diesel shunters which had still been carrying their old identities. Having arrived in 1971, it spent 8 ½ years as a Bradford loco before leaving for Healey Mills in September 1980. It ended its days at York and was scrapped in 1988. *(John Holroyd)*

This is Hall Lane crossing on 15 November 1983 - exactly ten years to the day after the view on the previous page. Much had changed, although it was the same dull weather! Hall Lane signalbox had closed on 27 March 1979 and was later demolished. For several months, the barriers were secured out of use in the raised position to permit free movement of road traffic. During this period, the McIntyre's scrap trains had to be flagged over the crossing under the supervision of railway staff. This temporary arrangement ended in August 1979 when barrier control pedestals were installed. These were activated with a key carried by the guard, who is seen here lowering the barriers as the return working from Laisterdyke to Springmill Street clears the crossing. On this day, the 1050 a.m. outward working to Laisterdyke had conveyed eight empty wagons. Nine loaded wagons were then collected for the return journey. The locomotive in charge was 08766, which had been on Hammerton Street's books since 1978 and remained there until the depot's closure in May 1984. *(Alan Whitaker)*

Back at Hall Lane in far better weather on 27 April 1984 and Bradford's last goods guard, Harry Nicholl, strolls up to activate the barriers as 08517 waits to cross with 12 empty wagons and a brake van bound for McIntyre's. These were the last regular duties of Harry's long railway career as he neared retirement. After almost 20 years' service in the North East, followed by a brief spell at Healey Mills, 08517 was transferred to Hammerton Street in October 1978 and remained part of the depot's allocation until closure in May 1984. It then migrated to Leeds Neville Hill with the rest of the displaced Bradford-based Class 08s. In later life, 08517 worked from Stratford depot in East London and during its time there, was selected as one of the dedicated shunting locomotives for Channel Tunnel construction works trains. These were renumbered for the duration and 08517 became RS077. It was finally withdrawn in 2001 after a service life of just under 43 years and scrapped after a period in store. *(Alan Whitaker)*

Guard Harry Nicholl seems to be in contemplative mood as he gazes from the rear veranda of his brake van, No. DB951856, on the 9K02 trip from Springmill Street to Laisterdyke on 27 April 1984. He would not be making this familiar journey many more times. The long straight between Hall Lane and Laisterdyke can be seen receding into the distance through the brake van's inner door. *(Alan Whitaker)*

With the Planetrees Road overbridge creating a fine backdrop, 08239 prepares to shunt five empty wagons into McIntyre's siding at Laisterdyle on Wednesday, 4 April 1984. McIntyre's yard occupied the former Planetrees goods depot site which had closed on 11 September 1961, although some accommodation was retained for coal wagons awaiting entry into the Birks Hall Gas Works sidings. Planetrees was the first of Laisterdyke's three ex-Great Northern Railway yards to close. The next was Quarry Gap in October 1968 and the East yard closed in August 1979. *(Steve Hall)*

The siding used for McIntyre's traffic was once part of a much longer line which continued to the Birks Hall Gas Works yard. Birks Hall opened in 1938 and burned coal to produce coke and coal gas. The plant had an insatiable appetite for coal and required a vast number of wagon loads from collieries all over Yorkshire to keep it fed. After operating at reduced capacity for a couple of years, the gas works closed in 1969 and was demolished in 1972/3. The long access siding was later cut back and continued in regular use until 1987, after which the scrap traffic became sporadic, then dried up completely. However, McIntyre's successor company reached agreement with BR to retain the siding connection as they had not ruled out using rail again. 08239 is seen here having placed empty wagons into the siding on 4 April 1984. *(Steve Hall)*

Having detached the brake van from the rear of their train, the crew of 9K02 pose alongside 08239 at Laisterdyke during a pause in shunting operations on the same day as the previous two views. From left to right, they are Driver Ronnie Speed, Guard Harry Nicholl (holding the shunting pole) and Secondman David Dobson. 08239 was the last Class 08 to be added to the Hammerton Street allocation, arriving from Stratford (London) in December 1982. Close inspection of the cabside reveals that the loco was still carrying its Stratford allocation sticker 16 months later! On closure of Hammerton Street depot just over six weeks after this view was captured, it was transferred to Leeds Neville Hill but did not leave Bradford immediately and was seen stabled at Mill Lane Junction on 21 May 1984 - a week after its official transfer date. Enquiries at the time suggested that it had been kept back for permanent-way work at Springmill Street. When it did finally go, it was not needed at its new home and was officially withdrawn on 8 July 1984. A long period of storage followed before it was finally cut up in 1996, 40 years after it was built. *(Steve Hall)*

Class 31s were the favoured motive power after Healey Mills took over the McIntyre's scrap workings from Monday, 14 May 1984, following the closure of Hammerton Street. After a stop for the barriers to be activated at Hall Lane level crossing, this unidentified example is seen heading along the Bowling Branch towards Laisterdyke with the morning empties in July 1984. *(Andrew Rapacz)*

31324 worked the morning trip from Healey Mills on 8 October 1984 and is seen here at Laisterdyke about to shunt 10 empty wagons into the scrap siding. The five loaded wagons at the rear of the train had already been collected and propelled back on to the shunt loop. This loop had been created in 1979 to streamline operations at Laisterdyke. As well as enabling locomotives to run-round, it provided 300 yards of standage which was more than enough as the McIntyre's trains rarely exceeded 12 wagons. A new trailing connection to provide access to McIntyre's siding from the Leeds-Bradford main line was installed in September 1985 and the branch to Bowling Junction was then closed. Track was lifted in March 1987. The original main line connection with the branch had been removed in July 1970 as part of track rationalisation in the Laisterdyke area and meant that the only access for McIntyre's traffic for the next 15 years was via Bowling Junction and Hall Lane. *(Gavin Morrison)*

Although still connected to the national network, the Laisterdyke scrap siding lay dormant for a number of years before the UK's biggest metal recycling company, European Metal Recyclers, took over the Planetrees Road operation. The company was keen to test its rail facility and, on 1 April 1998, a trial train was run from Liverpool Alexandra Dock, where EMR had another rail-connected site dealing with the export of scrap via the Port of Liverpool. This view, taken from Planetrees Road bridge, shows Class 37 No. 37716 about to propel the loaded wagons from the siding before heading down to Bradford Interchange where it would reverse before returning to Merseyside. After years of disuse, it would appear that the siding had been cleared of vegetation and 'fettled' in preparation for the arrival of the train. It also appears that a new bufferstop had been installed at the end of the siding and the perimeter wall of the scrapyard shows evidence of recent repairs. The locomotive was, at this time, operated by English, Welsh & Scottish Railways (EWS) and was evidently not long out of the paint shop. The trial train proved successful and led to the scrap metal traffic being revived as and when market conditions dictated. (Gavin Morrison)

Fluctuations in the value of exported scrap metal - particularly to the Chinese market - meant that it was difficult to predict when the scrap trains from Laisterdyke would run, and for how long. If economic conditions were favourable, they could run uninterrupted for long periods, then disappear for months - or even years. However, the EMR siding connection has been retained and maintained so rail operations can be re-started at fairly short notice. At the time of writing, there had not been any of these workings for several years but the company is keeping its options open and it is still possible that trains of scrap from Laisterdyke will be seen again in the coming years. This view shows EWS Class 66, No. 66179, setting out from Laisterdyke with a full load on 26 September 2000. *(Peter Holden)*

The Laisterdyke 'scrapper' descends from Wakefield Road Tunnel towards Usher Street bridge and St. Dunstan's on 16 April 2002, with Cardiff-based BR Class 56 No. 56048 in charge. Although part of the EWS fleet since 1995, the locomotive still sports its former BR Civil Engineers' Sector livery of grey and yellow. This was nicknamed 'Dutch' livery as it was very similar to that used by the Netherlands State Railways. Class 56s were regular performers on these trains in 2001/02 and became a familiar sight in Bradford Interchange station where they had to run round using one of the engine release lines. The trains then headed to Healey Mills via Halifax for a crew change before continuing to their ultimate destination. 56048 had only four more months of service left, being withdrawn in August 2002 after a service life of only 23 years. It was then sold for scrap – ironically to EMR who disposed of it in their yard at Kingsbury. *(Peter Holden)*

Class 56 heavy freight locomotives rarely had any need to visit Bradford Interchange until they began to appear on the Laisterdyke scrap workings in 2001/02. Prior to that, they occasionally turned up on weekend engineers' trains, as seen here on Sunday, 4 August 1996. Having been left idling for a while, 56067 opens up, leaving a fog of diesel exhaust in its wake as it lifts its load of permanent way wagons up the gradient towards Mill Lane Junction on its way back to Healey Mills. The locomotive is still carrying the 'triple grey' BR Coal Sector colours of its former owner. Its next repaint would be into the red and gold of EWS which had taken over freight operations from BR in 1995. 56067 was withdrawn in December 2003 and was one of a large number of redundant Class 56s held in store for several years at various locations up and down the country. It was sold for scrap in 2011 and taken by road from Crewe to a yard at Stockton-on-Tees where it was cut up. *(Gavin Morrison)*

A new operator appeared in Bradford in 2010 when Grand Central Trains introduced a direct service from Interchange station to London King's Cross. The company had been operating between Sunderland and King's Cross since 2007, using three second hand HSTs, but the Bradford services were implemented with five-car 125 m.p.h. Class 180 diesel hydraulic *Adelante* sets. These had originally been operated by First Great Western from 2000 until 2008 when they were returned to their leasing company. Grand Central now has 10 sets, with the other four in the fleet operated by Hull Trains. The Bradford to King's Cross service began on 23 May 2010, with stops at Halifax, Brighouse, Wakefield Kirkgate, Pontefract and Doncaster. A stop at Mirfield was introduced in December 2011 and the new station at Low Moor was added after its opening in 2017. A programme of refurbishment of Grand Central's Class 180s began in 2018. On 6 May 2011, 180105 lays over at Bradford Interchange after arrival from London. Five months later, this set was named in honour of the internationally famous Yorkshire artist, Ashley Jackson. *(Martin Bairstow)*

The award of the new Northern franchise to Arriva in 2016 came with a Department of Transport caveat to get rid of the ageing and unpopular Pacer trains by 2020 and replace them with new stock. The only manufacturer Arriva could find which could quickly supply both a diesel and electric train based the same overall design was the Spanish firm CAF. Orders were placed and the first Class 195 diesel unit arrived in the UK for testing in 2018. A total of 58 sets were ordered - 25 two-car and 33 three-car. The first entered service in July 2019 and they began to appear regularly on Calder Valley services between Manchester Victoria and Leeds via Bradford a few months later. A formation of two 3-car sets is seen here at Bradford Interchange on the delayed 1258 to Leeds on 1 November 2019. Class 331s - the electric version of the DMU design - were introduced on Airedale and Wharfedale services from Bradford Forster Square in September/October 2019. The arrival of the new trains was a bright spot in what had otherwise been a chastening experience for Arriva as the Northern franchise holder. Poor punctuality, industrial action and a farcical timetable launch backlash prompted the Government to strip it of its franchise and Northern Trains, a publicly-owned 'Operator of Last Resort,' took over on 1 March 2020. *(Iain Dickinson)*

Here's something worth getting up for early on a freezing winter day in the middle of a global pandemic! First generation diesel traction in normal service had become very rare in Bradford by 2021 but photographer Peter Holden knew that a Direct Rail Services Class 37 would be at Interchange station if he got there early enough. 37422 had been in West Yorkshire for a few days on winter railhead treatment duties and had even featured on the local BBC News while in action in the Huddersfield area. The venerable locomotive is seen here on the stabling siding at Bradford Interchange just before 7 a.m. on 7 February 2021. It is carrying the name *Victorious*, which is probably apt as it had survived against the odds and was still in main line service at the age of 56. 37422 started life as D6966 at Sheffield Darnall shed in February 1965. The key to its longevity came in 1986 when it was one of 31 Class 37s refurbished at Crewe Works and fitted with electric train heating equipment, thereby giving it a new lease of life. It passed into DRS ownership after the previous owner, DB Schenker, put all its Class 37/4s up for sale in 2010. DRS announced in 2020 that it would continue to run its remaining Class 37s – including 37422 – until 2025 so, barring a catastrophe, the locomotive should live to see its 60th birthday. *(Peter Holden)*